KOREAN
IMMIGRATION

Sheila Smith Noonan

THE CHANGING
Face of North America:
IMMIGRATION SINCE 1965

KOREAN
IMMIGRATION

Sheila Smith Noonan

MASON CREST PUBLISHERS
PHILADELPHIA

Produced by OTTN Publishing, Stockton, New Jersey

Mason Crest Publishers
370 Reed Road
Broomall, PA 19008
www.masoncrest.com

First printing

1 3 5 7 9 8 6 4 2

Library of Congress Cataloging-in-Publication Data

Noonan, Sheila Smith.
  Korean immigration / Sheila Smith Noonan.
    p. cm. — (The changing face of North America)
Summary: An overview of immigration from Korea to the United States and Canada since the 1960s, when immigration laws were changed to permit greater numbers of people to enter these countries.
Includes bibliographical references and index.
  ISBN 1-59084-693-1
  1. Korean Americans—History—20th century—Juvenile literature. 2. Koreans—Canada—History—20th century—Juvenile literature. 3. Immigrants—United States—History—20th century—Juvenile literature.
4. Immigrants—Canada—History—20th century—Juvenile literature. 5. Korea—Emigration and immigration—History—20th century—Juvenile literature. 6. United States—Emigration and immigration—History—20th century—Juvenile literature. 7. Canada—Emigration and immigration—History—20th century—Juvenile literature.
[1. Korean Americans—History—20th century. 2. Koreans—Canada—History—20th century. 3. Immigrants—United States—History—20th century. 4. Immigrants—Canada—History—20th century. 5. Korea—Emigration and immigration—History—20th century. 6. United States—Emigration and immigration—History—20th century. 7. Canada—Emigration and immigration—History—20th century.] I. Title. II. Changing face of North America.
  E184.K6N66 2004
  304.8'730519—dc22

                                                      2003013259

THE **CHANGING**
Face of North America:
IMMIGRATION SINCE 1965

CONTENTS

INTRODUCTION

THE CHANGING FACE OF AMERICA

By Senator Edward M. Kennedy

America is proud of its heritage and history as a nation of immigrants, and my own family is an example. All eight of my great-grandparents were immigrants who left Ireland a century and a half ago, when that land was devastated by the massive famine caused by the potato blight. When I was a young boy, my grandfather used to take me down to the docks in Boston and regale me with stories about the Great Famine and the waves of Irish immigrants who came to America seeking a better life. He talked of how the Irish left their marks in Boston and across the nation, enduring many hardships and harsh discrimination, but also building the railroads, digging the canals, settling the West, and filling the factories of a growing America. According to one well-known saying of the time, "under every railroad tie, an Irishman is buried."

America was the promised land for them, as it has been for so many other immigrants who have found shelter, hope, opportunity, and freedom. Immigrants have always been an indispensable part of our nation. They have contributed immensely to our communities, created new jobs and whole new industries, served in our armed forces, and helped make America the continuing land of promise that it is today.

The inspiring poem by Emma Lazarus, inscribed on the pedestal of the Statue of Liberty in New York Harbor, is America's welcome to all immigrants:

Give me your tired, your poor,
Your huddled masses yearning to breathe free,
The wretched refuse of your teeming shore,
Send these, the homeless, tempest-tossed, to me:
I lift my lamp beside the golden door.

The period since September 11, 2001, has been particularly challenging for immigrants. Since the horrifying terrorist attacks, there has been a resurgence of anti-immigrant attitudes and behavior. We all agree that our borders must be safe and secure. Yet, at the same time, we must safeguard the entry of the millions of persons who come to the United States legally each year as immigrants, visitors, scholars, students, and workers. The "golden door" must stay open. We must recognize that immigration is not the problem—terrorism is. We must identify and isolate the terrorists, and not isolate America.

One of my most important responsibilities in the Senate is the preservation of basic rights and basic fairness in the application of our immigration laws, so that new generations of immigrants in our own time and for all time will have the same opportunity that my great-grandparents had when they arrived in America.

Immigration is beneficial for the United States and for countries throughout the world. It is no coincidence that two hundred years ago, our nations' founders chose *E Pluribus Unum*—"out of many, one"—as America's motto. These words, chosen by Benjamin Franklin, John Adams, and Thomas Jefferson, refer to the ideal that separate colonies can be transformed into one united nation. Today, this ideal has come to apply to individuals as well. Our diversity is our strength. We are a nation of immigrants, and we always will be.

FOREWORD

THE CHANGING FACE OF THE UNITED STATES

Marian L. Smith, historian
U.S. Immigration and Naturalization Service

Americans commonly assume that immigration today is very different than immigration of the past. The immigrants themselves appear to be unlike immigrants of earlier eras. Their language, their dress, their food, and their ways seem strange. At times people fear too many of these new immigrants will destroy the America they know. But has anything really changed? Do new immigrants have any different effect on America than old immigrants a century ago? Is the American fear of too much immigration a new development? Do immigrants really change America more than America changes the immigrants? The very subject of immigration raises many questions.

In the United States, immigration is more than a chapter in a history book. It is a continuous thread that links the present moment to the first settlers on North American shores. From the first colonists' arrival until today, immigrants have been met by Americans who both welcomed and feared them. Immigrant contributions were always welcome—on the farm, in the fields, and in the factories. Welcoming the poor, the persecuted, and the "huddled masses" became an American principle. Beginning with the original Pilgrims' flight from religious persecution in the 1600s, through the Irish migration to escape starvation in the 1800s, to the relocation of Central Americans seeking refuge from civil wars in the 1980s and 1990s, the United States has considered itself a haven for the destitute and the oppressed.

But there was also concern that immigrants would not adopt American ways, habits, or language. Too many immigrants might overwhelm America. If so, the dream of the Founding Fathers for United States government and society would be destroyed. For this reason, throughout American history some have argued that limiting or ending immigration is our patriotic duty. Benjamin Franklin feared there were so many German immigrants in Pennsylvania the Colonial Legislature would begin speaking German. "Progressive" leaders of the early 1900s feared that immigrants who could not read and understand the English language were not only exploited by "big business," but also served as the foundation for "machine politics" that undermined the U.S. Constitution. This theme continues today, usually voiced by those who bear no malice toward immigrants but who want to preserve American ideals.

Have immigrants changed? In colonial days, when most colonists were of English descent, they considered Germans, Swiss, and French immigrants as different. They were not "one of us" because they spoke a different language. Generations later, Americans of German or French descent viewed Polish, Italian, and Russian immigrants as strange. They were not "like us" because they had a different religion, or because they did not come from a tradition of constitutional government. Recently, Americans of Polish or Italian descent have seen Nicaraguan, Pakistani, or Vietnamese immigrants as too different to be included. It has long been said of American immigration that the latest ones to arrive usually want to close the door behind them.

It is important to remember that fear of individual immigrant groups seldom lasted, and always lessened. Benjamin Franklin's anxiety over German immigrants disappeared after those immigrants' sons and daughters helped the nation gain independence in the Revolutionary War. The Irish of the mid-1800s were among the most hated immigrants, but today we all wear green on St. Patrick's Day. While a century ago it was feared that Italian and other Catholic immigrants would vote as directed by the Pope, today that controversy is only a vague memory. Unfortunately, some ethnic groups continue their efforts to earn acceptance. The African Americans' struggle continues, and some Asian Americans, whose families have been in America for generations, are the victims of current anti-immigrant sentiment.

Time changes both immigrants and America. Each wave of new immigrants, with their strange language and habits, eventually grows old and passes away. Their American-born children speak English. The immigrants' grandchildren are completely American. The strange foods of their ancestors—spaghetti, baklava, hummus, or tofu—become common in any American restaurant or grocery store. Much of what the immigrants brought to these shores is lost, principally their language. And what is gained becomes as American as St. Patrick's Day, Hanukkah, or Cinco de Mayo, and we forget that it was once something foreign.

Recent immigrants are all around us. They come from every corner of the earth to join in the American Dream. They will continue to help make the American Dream a reality, just as all the immigrants who came before them have done.

THE CHANGING FACE OF CANADA

Peter A. Hammerschmidt
First Secretary, Permanent Mission of Canada to the United Nations

Throughout Canada's history, immigration has shaped and defined the very character of Canadian society. The migration of peoples from every part of the world into Canada has profoundly changed the way we look, speak, eat, and live. Through close and distant relatives who left their lands in search of a better life, all Canadians have links to immigrant pasts. We are a nation built by and of immigrants.

Two parallel forces have shaped the history of Canadian immigration. The enormous diversity of Canada's immigrant population is the most obvious. In the beginning came the enterprising settlers of the "New World," the French and English colonists. Soon after came the Scottish, Irish, and Northern and Central European farmers of the 1700s and 1800s. As the country expanded westward during the mid-1800s, migrant workers began arriving from China, Japan, and other Asian countries. And the turbulent twentieth century brought an even greater variety of immigrants to Canada, from the Caribbean, Africa, India, and Southeast Asia.

So while English- and French-Canadians are the largest ethnic groups in the country today, neither group alone represents a majority of the population. A large and vibrant multicultural mix makes up the rest, particularly in Canada's major cities. Toronto, Vancouver, and Montreal alone are home to people from over 200 ethnic groups!

Less obvious but equally important in the evolution of Canadian immigration has been hope. The promise of a better life lured

Europeans and Americans seeking cheap (sometimes even free) farmland. Thousands of Scots and Irish arrived to escape grinding poverty and starvation. Others came for freedom, to escape religious and political persecution. Canada has long been a haven to the world's dispossessed and disenfranchised—Dutch and German farmers cast out for their religious beliefs, black slaves fleeing the United States, and political refugees of despotic regimes in Europe, Africa, Asia, and South America.

The two forces of diversity and hope, so central to Canada's past, also shaped the modern era of Canadian immigration. Following the Second World War, Canada drew heavily on these influences to forge trailblazing immigration initiatives.

The catalyst for change was the adoption of the Canadian Bill of Rights in 1960. Recognizing its growing diversity and Canadians' changing attitudes towards racism, the government passed a federal statute barring discrimination on the grounds of race, national origin, color, religion, or sex. Effectively rejecting the discriminatory elements in Canadian immigration policy, the Bill of Rights forced the introduction of a new policy in 1962. The focus of immigration abruptly switched from national origin to the individual's potential contribution to Canadian society. The door to Canada was now open to every corner of the world.

Welcoming those seeking new hopes in a new land has also been a feature of Canadian immigration in the modern era. The focus on economic immigration has increased along with Canada's steadily growing economy, but political immigration has also been encouraged. Since 1945, Canada has admitted tens of thousands of displaced persons, including Jewish Holocaust survivors, victims of Soviet crackdowns in Hungary and Czechoslovakia, and refugees from political upheaval in Uganda, Chile, and Vietnam.

Prior to 1978, however, these political refugees were admitted as an exception to normal immigration procedures. That year, Canada revamped its refugee policy with a new Immigration Act that explicitly affirmed Canada's commitment to the resettlement of refugees from oppression. Today, the admission of refugees remains a central part of Canadian immigration law and regulations.

Amendments to economic and political immigration policy continued during the 1980s and 1990s, refining further the bold steps taken during the modern era. Together, these initiatives have turned Canada into one of the world's few truly multicultural states.

Unlike the process of assimilation into a "melting pot" of cultures, immigrants to Canada are more likely to retain their cultural identity, beliefs, and practices. This is the source of some of Canada's greatest strengths as a society. And as a truly multicultural nation, diversity is not seen as a threat to Canadian identity. Quite the contrary—diversity *is* Canadian identity.

1

Newcomers to America's Melting Pot

The Korean Peninsula, located south of China in eastern Asia, is home to about 70 million people. In addition, nearly 6 million ethnic Koreans live in countries around the globe, having gone from native sons and daughters to newcomers, from majority to minority. Of this group, about 1.2 million have settled in the United States, and nearly 150,000 call Canada their home.

Compared with Europeans and even some Asian immigrant groups such as the Japanese, Koreans are relatively new arrivals to the United States and Canada. The 100th anniversary of Korean immigration to the United States was celebrated in 2003: on January 13, 1903, a ship carrying 102 Korean men, women, and children landed in Hawaii, which was then a U.S. possession. These first Korean Americans had crossed the Pacific Ocean to work on Hawaii's sugar plantations.

Korean migration to America slowed to a trickle during the first half of the 20th century. In 1905 Korea became a protectorate of Japan, which restricted emigration from the peninsula; for its part, the U.S. government, through the Immigration Act of 1924, essentially barred Koreans and other Asians from immigrating to the United States. The War Brides Act of 1945, designed to reunite American servicemen with foreign-born wives and children, permitted more Koreans to enter.

Twenty years later, the Immigration Act of 1965 removed quotas that kept Koreans and other Asians from entering the

◀ Koreans are relative newcomers to the United States and Canada: the first official immigrants from the Korean Peninsula—102 agricultural workers and their families—arrived in Hawaii on January 13, 1903. This hand-tinted photograph shows three early Korean migrants on the deck of a ship.

United States in significant numbers. Similarly, a more liberal immigration policy in Canada, enacted in 1962 and 1967, enabled Koreans and people from other underrepresented ethnic groups to live there. (Unless otherwise noted, in this book the term *Koreans*, when used in reference to recent immigration from the Korean Peninsula, signifies people from South Korea, which has elected leaders and an open immigration policy. By contrast, Communist North Korea has closed borders, and very few people manage to leave.)

Unity and Diversity

Koreans, unlike citizens of many Western countries, are a homogeneous group. Except for very small communities of ethnic Chinese and Japanese, everyone on the Korean Peninsula shares Korean ancestry. But that's not to say there isn't a great deal of diversity within the Korean American community. In education, political views, and religious beliefs, for example, Korean Americans represent a full range of experiences and opinions. Even attitudes toward their adopted home differ greatly across the Korean American community. Authors Elaine H. Kim and Eui-Young Yu interviewed Korean Americans from all walks of life for their book *East to America*. They observed, "Despite their national and cultural affinities, which are sometimes intensified by feelings of displacement, there are important generational, gender, and class distinctions, each formed within the other. To some of the people we interviewed, America is a sanctuary, a promised land. To some, it is purgatory. To others, it has been a prison. And to still others, it is the only home they have ever known."

The first post-1965 Korean immigrants to the United States arrived in a land that was tense and divided over black and white racial issues. The ability of America's melting pot to accept Koreans and other ethnic groups—whose numbers soon swelled—would once again be put to the test. For some Koreans, that pot would slowly simmer and then roar to a boil in Los Angeles in 1992 with racial tensions and conflict.

For many years, Korean Americans were widely viewed as a "model minority": academic overachievers and introverts, quiet, submissive, and hardworking. Indeed, in major cities a significant number of Korean immigrants opened small businesses, such as green groceries, that required them to work 14 or more hours a day, seven days a week. It is also true that Korean parents placed a high value on education. However, these stereotypes—along with a language barrier and a tendency for Koreans to keep to themselves, especially in the early years—contributed to a gulf between people born in Korea and people whose ancestors came to America generations earlier.

Koreans and Asian Americans

The number of Korean immigrants to the United States swelled in the 1980s and has since tapered off, but they still belong to one of the fastest-growing ethnic groups in America, Asian Americans. According to U.S. Census Bureau projections, approximately 34 million Asian Americans will live in the United States by 2050.

Canada has emerged as a leading destination for Korean emigrants. The Canadian government views immigration as crucial to the country's future. In April 2002, the Honorable Denis Coderre, minister of citizenship and immigration, said, "Canada needs immigrants if it is to continue to grow and prosper."

Throughout this book, reference will be made to three groups of Korean Americans: the first generation, the 1.5 generation, and the second generation. While in standard American usage the term *first generation* refers to children born in the country to which their parents immigrated, Korean Americans (as well as some other Asian immigrants) use the term differently. To them, a first-generation Korean American is someone born on the Korean Peninsula who immigrated to North America as an adult. In this book, that is the sense in which the term will be used. The 1.5 generation was born in Korea but emigrated (usually with their parents) when they were children or young teenagers. The second generation refers to Koreans born in the United States or Canada to parents who had emigrated from the peninsula. Each generation has unique characteristics and its own perspective on what it is like to be a Korean American or Canadian.

For research and statistical purposes, Korean Americans often are included with people of Asian heritage: Chinese, Hmong, Vietnamese, Japanese, Filipinos, and others. In everyday life, Korean Americans (and people from other Asian nations) would like to be considered as individuals. Their history, culture, and experiences are unique, not to be blurred with those of any other Asian country. In *Becoming Asian American*, author Nazli Kibria relates the story of a Korean American named Eugene, who often was mistaken for being Japanese American. Eugene said, "Someone makes a negative comment about the Japanese for their economic politics, and they look at me to see if I'm offended . . . I don't just stand there and take it like some silent Asian. I say, 'I'm Korean. I'm Korean.' And don't you know that Koreans despise the Japanese for the way we were treated by them?'"

Korean Americans often are asked, "Where are you from?" For some, it is a loaded question, however innocently asked, that sets them apart as outsiders. One woman interviewed in *Becoming Asian American* shapes her response to educate those who ask. "I think it's really important for people to realize that we're not foreigners," she believes. "That's a really big misconception because I get the question all the time: 'Where are you from?' And it hurts me, it offends me. People probably think I'm nitpicking and paranoid, but lately I say, 'Excuse me, I think what you mean is 'What is your ethnicity?' As far as my nationality, I'm a U.S. citizen. As far as my ethnicity, I'm a Korean American."

Many Americans and Canadians never have experienced the phenomenon of being immigrants because their ancestors made the journey generations ago. Although the times have changed,

Following in His Parents' Footsteps

Jay H. Chung came to the United States when he was 11, joining his parents, who had emigrated years earlier. Prospects were bleak for his family in Korea for political reasons. "My grandfather was minister of defense when the government he was serving was overthrown," says Chung. "With him under house arrest and my father, an accountant, unable to get a job, our options were not great."

Chung's mother, a microbiologist, was the first of the family to leave Korea, pursuing her doctorate at the University of Wisconsin. She emigrated when Chung was four, and two years later, his father joined her. When Chung and his younger brother came to the United States in 1969, the transition was difficult, but not just because he didn't speak English. "My grandmother raised me in a separate house from my parents since I was a toddler, so my parents were in many ways strangers to me," says Chung. "My first year in America was unsettling. I had to learn a new language, meet a new sister, and adapt to a new culture. Fortunately, my parents were quite progressive and Americanized, and after a short time, I was able to excel in school and extra-curricular activities, including sports." Most important, his grandmother came to America, too, which was "a comforting event."

Like his mother, Chung had a love and aptitude for science. He studied electrical engineering and biology at the Massachusetts Institute of Technology and then earned a medical degree and a doctorate at Harvard Medical School. Today, he is a cancer researcher at the National Institutes of Health, where both his mother and his wife also work.

all immigrants leave something behind: loved ones, friends, jobs. They come in search of a new life. In a speech before the Daughters of the American Revolution in 1936, President Franklin D. Roosevelt said, "Remember, remember always, that all of us, and you and I especially, are descended from immigrants and revolutionists."

2 THE COUNTRY THEY LEFT BEHIND

Throughout history, the Korean Peninsula has been invaded and occupied by foreigners, including the Chinese, Mongols, and Japanese. In the early 20th century Japan ruled Korea as a protectorate, then annexed the peninsula, making it a part of the expanding Japanese empire.

In August 1945, when Japan surrendered to end World War II, the peninsula was hastily divided into two occupation zones: the American zone, south of the 38th parallel, and the Soviet zone, north of the 38th parallel. This partition was intended as a temporary measure, to facilitate the orderly surrender of Japanese troops in Korea. But as relations between the United States and the Soviet Union deteriorated at the beginning of the period that came to be called the Cold War, plans to unify Korea stalled. By late summer of 1948 two opposing governments had been proclaimed: the Republic of Korea (South Korea), which was supported by the United States; and the Democratic People's Republic of Korea (North Korea), a Soviet-backed Communist regime.

The Korean War

By June 1949 the United States had withdrawn its troops from South Korea. A year later, on June 25, 1950, North Korean troops streamed across the 38th parallel in a surprise attack that overwhelmed the South Korean armed forces. Within four days, South Korea's capital, Seoul, had fallen.

◀ Built during the late 14th century A.D. by King T'aejo, the founder of Korea's Choson dynasty (1392–1910), the palace complex of Kyongbokkung was destroyed during a 16th-century Japanese invasion but later restored. Throughout its history, Korea has been invaded and occupied by a succession of foreigners, including the Chinese, Mongols, and Japanese.

President Harry S. Truman quickly committed U.S. forces to counter the invasion, and more than a dozen United Nations member countries—including Great Britain, Australia, and Canada—later joined the American military effort. By August 1950, however, the North Koreans were in control of the entire peninsula with the exception of a small perimeter around the southeastern city of Pusan. But on September 15, U.S. forces landed at Inchon, well behind North Korean lines. Over the ensuing weeks, American, South Korean, and U.N. troops steadily pushed the North Korean army back. Then, in late October, as the front approached the Yalu River—which marks the border between North Korea and the Peoples Republic of China—Communist China entered the war on the side of North Korea. The Soviet Union also committed forces to aid the North.

An artillery unit lights up the night near Seoul, 1950. The Korean War, which began on June 25, 1950, when North Korean units launched a surprise attack across the 38th parallel, lasted three years and devastated the peninsula.

With about 1,265 people per square mile, South Korea is one of the world's most densely populated countries. Shown here is the city of Cheju, located on an island in the East China Sea.

Over the next three years, uncommonly bitter and destructive fighting raged across the peninsula as the lines shifted with a string of bloody offensives and counteroffensives. By the time a cease-fire was signed on July 27, 1953, Korea was in ruins and a staggering number of people had lost their lives: about 4 million Koreans, many of them civilians, had been killed, as had approximately 1 million Chinese soldiers, 55,000 American troops, and about 500 Canadian military personnel.

Technically, North and South Korea are still at war, as no peace treaty has ever been concluded. Today the two countries are separated by a 2.4-mile-wide demilitarized zone that curves across the peninsula at about the 38th parallel. Though South Korea's president Kim Dae-jung and North Korean leader Kim Jong-il held direct talks in June 2000, relations have remained tense. North and South Korea have followed dramatically different courses since 1953, and when—or if—they will reunite remains unclear.

South Korea: Economic and Political Progress Amid Continuing Challenges

South Korea is a rugged land with many mountains and hills. It is also a densely populated country: in total area South Korea is only slightly larger than the state of Indiana, but it is home to almost eight times as many people. The capital city of

Seoul, with a population of nearly 10 million, is a blend of ancient treasures and modern sophistication.

Despite periodic setbacks, South Korea by the first decade of the 21st century has emerged as an economically prosperous and politically stable country. In 2001, according to the World Bank, it boasted the world's 13th-largest economy. Constitutional reforms enacted in 1987 gave Korean citizens the right to choose their president through direct elections, ensured a robust legislature, and strengthened civil rights.

Conditions were much different in the decade following the Korean War. Economically devastated, South Korea relied heavily on the United States for financial aid. Even with that help, "life for so many was the daily struggle for food," writes author Michael Breen in *The Koreans: Who They Are, What They Want, Where Their Future Lies.* "Until the early 1960s, peasants boiled grass and tree bark to make it through the spring when the barley crop was harvested." Breen notes that in the nation's early years, the South Korean government's

President Syngman Rhee held power in South Korea from 1948 until 1960, when he was ousted in a coup. Corruption and the suppression of civil liberties were hallmarks of his regime.

Two views of Seoul. South Korea's capital, a bustling metropolis of more than 9.6 million inhabitants, reflects the remarkable economic growth the nation enjoyed during the latter decades of the 20th century.

economic management was "hopelessly ignorant, short sighted, and corrupt."

The political situation was similarly disheartening. Although South Korea had some of the outward structures of democracy, Syngman Rhee—a corrupt and authoritarian ruler—clung to power from 1948 until 1960 through increasingly repressive means. Coups d'etat (violent takeovers of the government by the military) occurred in 1960 and 1961 (and again in 1980).

Despite South Korea's volatile politics, the country's economic picture steadily improved during the mid-1960s and the 1970s. As a farming society was transformed into a modern, industrialized nation, a middle class emerged—a novelty for class-conscious Koreans.

By the 1980s South Korea had emerged as one of the so-called Asian Tigers—four countries whose powerhouse economies, driven by exports, were growing at astonishing rates. South Korea claimed the world's eighth-largest economy by the mid-1990s. But beginning in 1997, a financial crisis rocked East Asia. As its stock market crashed, the value of its currency plummeted, and many of its companies faltered,

South Korean president Kim Dae-jung, winner of the 2000 Nobel Peace Prize, shakes hands with well-wishers in Seoul. The Nobel Committee, which cited Kim's work "for peace and reconciliation with North Korea," declared, "There may now be hope that the cold war will also come to an end in Korea." But such optimism soon faded, and relations between North and South Korea remain tense.

South Korea seemed on the brink of disaster. But with the help of economic reforms and a $58 billion loan from the International Monetary Fund, the country's economy stabilized and then rebounded.

Today, many of South Korea's manufactured products are familiar to American consumers—among them Hyundai and Kia automobiles and Daewoo electronics. By 2003 South Korea was the seventh-largest trading partner of the United States.

Politically, South Korea has made remarkable progress in the half century since the Korean War, but significant challenges remain. While the constitutional reform of 1987 helped ensure a more open electoral process and a more responsive govern-ment, political corruption remains a concern. Scandals have marred the careers of several prominent Korean politicians. Even the historic reunification talks between North Korea and South Korea in 2000, for which former South Korean president Kim Dae-jung received the Nobel Peace Prize, have been tainted by accusations that the meetings were "bought" with payments to North Korea of $192 million by Hyundai Merchant Marine.

In addition, despite its commitment to creating a free and democratic society, South Korea's record on human rights falls short in some areas. In its 2001 report on human rights practices in South Korea, the U.S. Department of State notes that "the Government generally respects the human rights of its citizens; however, problems remain in some areas such as police brutality and freedom of expression." The source of many of these problems can be traced to one piece of Korean legislation, the National Security Law of 1948. The government has used this law to silence criticism of its policies; artists and writers, political activists, and students are under close scrutiny by officials. South Korean authorities are especially sensitive when it

A Complex Chapter

It's when Sun Yung Shin is around first-generation Korean Americans that the thought, however fleeting, sometimes surfaces: "I'm not Korean enough for them."

Born in Seoul, South Korea, Shin was legally abandoned at a police station as an infant. She was adopted by an American couple, grew up in Brookfield, Illinois, with an older brother who was adopted domestically, and was naturalized as a U.S. citizen in 1979. As a child, Shin had friends and a cousin who were also Korean adoptees, but there wasn't a Korean community from which to learn the language or culture. At 13, however, she went with chaperones and other Korean adoptees to Korea. "There were obvious differences between us and the Korean girls our age. We were much louder, boisterous, and taller than they," says Shin, now a poet, educator, and author of a children's book, *Cooper and Mr. Rhee*. "We also had freedoms that they didn't. It was eye-opening."

Like many of her second-generation Korean American friends, Shin feels there's a cultural and generation gap separating her from "Korean Koreans." And yet, as an adoptee, she has a unique role in the Korean immigration story. "Being a Korean adoptee," she says, "is an ongoing, complicated gift."

comes to matters involving North Korea. Watchdog organizations are concerned that people arrested for violating the National Security Law are not treated fairly and are denied some of their basic rights as Korean citizens.

Why They Emigrate

The motivations for Koreans to leave their homeland are varied and often complex—and to a certain extent they have changed over time. Like members of other immigrant groups, however, many Koreans have been searching for a better education, a better job, a better financial future, or a better life for their children.

While Koreans with family members in the United States gained the opportunity to immigrate after 1965, certain middle-class professionals, such as doctors and nurses, also came to America. Ironically, this was attributable in part to South Korea's success in establishing a first-rate educational and professional training system. As anthropologist Kyeyoung Park explains in her book *The Korean American Dream*, "On the one hand, U.S. government policies allowed the Korean middle class, not the poor, to emigrate; on the other hand, the Korean government was not able to absorb its mass-produced professional managerial class. Many emigrants left Korea in pursuit of mobility and modernity and felt that these aspirations could

Since the mid-1960s, businesspeople have figured prominently among South Korean immigrants to the United States and Canada. With its first-rate educational system, South Korea produces a large pool of highly qualified professionals, but the country's workforce is unable to absorb all of them.

be better achieved in the American labor market." Other motivators for leaving Korea included the unstable domestic political scene, concerns about invasion by North Korea, and what Park describes as "American fever"—the strong economic, political, and cultural influence of the United States.

Some Koreans come to the United States or Canada for something that is highly valued in their homeland: a college education. During the 1996–97 academic year, there were about 37,000 Korean college students in the United States. Moon Jo, in his book *Korean Immigrants and the Challenge of Adjustment*, describes several reasons why an overseas education might be attractive to Korean students and their families: lower costs at American colleges for education of equal quality to what's available in Korea; the ability to study subjects unavailable in their homeland; and the possibility of better jobs in Korea-based American firms for Korean graduates of American colleges. One student Jo interviewed came to the United States because of inadequate research facilities in Korea, but after completing his studies, he brought his children over for their education. "Although I am no longer in [an] academic line of work—in fact I am a gardener—I am happy because my children are getting an excellent education at the University of California," he said.

Once a college degree is earned, the next logical step is to get a job. In Korea, that's not always as easy as writing a résumé, filling out an application, and going on job interviews. The competition for jobs in Korea is fierce; there are many more qualified applicants than positions. Even after someone has landed a job, promotions and salary raises can be slow in coming.

The American Dream—that anyone who works hard can succeed in business—is attractive to Koreans who have little hope for career advancement in their country. Yet this dream is not always fulfilled. "It is not unusual to find that the owner of a small store, a gardener, a cab driver, and a restaurant employee were all college graduates and had held middle level or higher management positions in Korea," notes Jo.

Uma A. Segal, in *A Framework for Immigration*, suggests that two American imports influenced early Korean immigration to the United States: the American military and television. "The strong U.S. military presence in Korea," Segal writes, "increased the attraction of the United States in a number of ways. Intermarriage between U.S. servicemen and Korean women led to the emigration of more than 3,000 women annually in the 1970s and 1980s. Furthermore, the availability of U.S. television propagating the lifestyle of this nation caught the attention of middle-class Koreans, making them aware that the quality of life in the United States was preferable to that which they had at home."

About 10 percent of Korean Americans had no say in whether they wanted to immigrate to the United States. They were adopted as infants or young children. Korean adoptions

Amerasian babies were one result of the U.S. military presence in South Korea. Americans adopted many of these babies, as well as others who were orphaned or abandoned during the difficult economic times that followed the Korean War. Approximately 10 percent of all Korean Americans are adoptees.

began after the Korean War; many of the adopted children were born to Korean mothers and now-absent Western military fathers. Even after "war babies" were placed in American and European homes, Korean adoptions continued. Between 1955 and 1998, about 98,000 Korean children were adopted by American families.

For Koreans—living in a society that frowned on domestic adoptions (although a 1996 law now encourages them), that offered little support for single mothers, that stigmatized out-of-wedlock children, and that encouraged reduction in family size (invoking a "one-child" policy in 1986)— international adoption was an acceptable, if often difficult, choice. Some mothers simply wanted better lives for their children than they thought Korea could offer.

Jennifer Yang Hee Arndt, an adopted Korean American, grew up in the Midwest with her parents, two brothers, and a sister, who was also adopted from Korea. She loves her family, but she was raised in a world that was "very 'white.' I had little exposure to Korean things, although I went to Korean culture camp," says Arndt. "As I teenager, I resented my Asian identity."

College often changes people, and it had that effect on Arndt. Through conversations with professors, by attending college classes, and even by watching the movie *The Joy Luck Club*, the epic story of Chinese immigrant mothers and their American daughters, she worked out emotions about her adoption for the first time. In the film, there is a scene in which a mother tearfully abandons two babies by a tree. "That hit me like a freight train, because my mother abandoned me," says Arndt, noting that although the practice was legal, she saw, through the film, that it was also painful. "The movie changed my life."

In 1996 Arndt went to Korea in search of her birth family. She knew it was a long shot because she had little documentation. A filmmaker, she recorded her experience—and those of other Korean adoptees on a similar quest—in a documentary titled *Crossing Chasms*. Arndt persevered in the face of bureaucratic dead ends, and eventually, through media coverage, a woman came forward who believed she might be Arndt's mother. Their conversation was limited because of the language barrier, but a potential brother showed her family pictures. Finally, the woman and Arndt had blood drawn for DNA testing. They were not related.

"For some Korean adoptees, finding their birth parents becomes all-consuming," says Arndt. "I decided to let it go. Through the experience, however, I began to know myself better. The act of trying to find my birth mother has brought emotional closure."

North of the 38th Parallel

North Korea borders three countries—China, South Korea, and Russia—but it is one of the most isolated nations in the world. The Communist country, with a population of about 22 million, is led by the repressive, heavy-handed Kim Jong-il, who took over following the death of his father, Kim Il-sung, in 1994.

North Korea has been at odds with the United States since the Korean War. A relatively small U.S. force (about 37,000 troops as of 2003) remains in South Korea as part of a joint defense treaty designed primarily to deter North Korean aggression. It is understood that any attack across the 38th parallel will trigger a full response by the U.S. military.

Fortunately, the situation has never come to that, but over the years various incidents have ratcheted up the tension between North Korea and the United States. In 1968, for example, North Korea seized the U.S. ship *Pueblo* and held more than 80 crewmen captive for 11 months; the North Koreans claimed that the vessel had violated their territorial waters.

Perhaps the most serious flare-up of U.S.–North Korea tensions, however, began in the fall of 2002, when North Korea admitted that it had an active nuclear-weapons program. This was in violation of an agreement, signed in 1994, by which North Korea had promised to abandon its pursuit of nuclear weapons in return for economic and humanitarian aid from

Though he governs North Korea with an iron fist, Kim Jong-il likes to be known by the title "Dear Leader." Five decades of repressive Communist rule under Kim and his father, Kim Il-sung, have profoundly isolated and impoverished North Korea. Per-capita income south of the 38th parallel is 20 times higher, and relief agencies believe that 500,000 to 3 million North Koreans may have died of starvation since the 1990s.

other countries. In response to the revelations, the U.S. administration of President George W. Bush suspended fuel shipments to North Korea and spoke of possible military options. Earlier Bush had referred to North Korea as being part of an "axis of evil" and criticized its leader, Kim Jong-il, for being one who "starves his folks." South Korea stepped forward in an attempt to resolve the growing international crisis, acting as an unofficial mediator between its ally and its northern neighbor.

A very small number of people safely leave Communist North Korea each year as refugees; in 2001, according to the Asia Society, 583 refugees arrived in South Korea. Thousands of North Koreans try to escape to South Korea by way of China, but this is a very risky proposition. When captured by the Chinese, some are sent to prisons or work camps; there have been reports that others have been executed.

Given the living conditions for typical citizens in North Korea, some consider the attempt to escape to freedom (and possibly be reunited with relatives in South Korea) worth the risk of imprisonment or death. A sign on a building in Pyongyang, North Korea's capital city, reads, "We are happy." Author Michael Breen writes, "North Korea's regime exists on the lie that it has built a Worker's Paradise, an ideal society."

Human rights organizations find nothing ideal about the famine that, according to the U.S. State Department, has caused the death of about one million people (estimates from some relief agencies are even higher) from starvation and hunger-related diseases since 1994, nor the abuses that North Koreans endure each day. According to a June 2002 report from the British Broadcasting Corporation, more than half of the North Korean population is malnourished, some of them resorting to eating grass to survive.

Dr. Norbert Vollertsen, a German physician, was in North Korea from July 1999 to December 2000 on a humanitarian mission. In testimony to the United States Senate Committee on the Judiciary in June 2002, he described what he observed in North Korea. "There are two worlds in North Korea. The world for the senior military, the members of the workers party and the country's elite, where they are enjoying a nice lifestyle

Presidents George W. Bush of the United States and Roh Moo-hyun of South Korea strike a cordial pose for photographers after a meeting at the White House, May 14, 2003. But the two leaders disagreed over how to deal with North Korea and its nuclear-weapons program.

with fancy restaurants, diplomatic shops with European food, nightclubs, and even a casino. In the world for . . . ordinary people in a hospital, one can see young children, all of them too small for their age, with hollow eyes and skin stretched tight across their faces, wearing blue-and-white striped pajamas like the children in Auschwitz and Dachau in Hitler's Nazi Germany." The doctor said he was expelled from the country for "publicly denouncing the regime for abusing basic human rights and for its failure to distribute the massive foreign food aid to the people who needed it most."

3 THE CENTURY OF THE TIGER

Immigration from the Korean Peninsula to North America has come in three main waves. In the United States, those waves occurred during a span of 100 years, which some dubbed the Century of the Tiger. In Korean mythology, the tiger god exists in two worlds: spiritual and earthly. Fittingly, Korean immigrants to America have lived in two worlds also.

To better comprehend the three waves of Korean immigration to the United States, it helps to understand the history of U.S. immigration.

A Short History of U.S. Immigration to the Present Day

Immigration to the United States has been characterized by openness punctuated by periods of restriction. During the 17th, 18th, and 19th centuries, immigration was essentially open without restriction, and, at times, immigrants were even recruited to come to America. Between 1783 and 1820, approximately 250,000 immigrants arrived at U.S. shores. Between 1841 and 1860, more than 4 million immigrants came; most were from England, Ireland, and Germany.

Historically, race and ethnicity have played a role in legislation to restrict immigration. The Chinese Exclusion Act of 1882, which was not repealed until 1943, specifically prevented Chinese people from becoming U.S. citizens and did not allow Chinese laborers to immigrate for the next decade. An

◀ In the first 100 years of Korean immigration to North America, more than 900,000 people crossed the Pacific to make Canada or the United States their new home. These Koreans, dressed in traditional garb, were photographed around 1910.

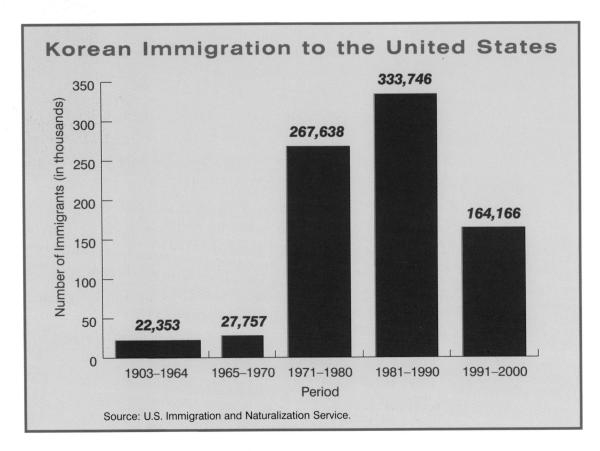

Korean Immigration to the United States

Number of Immigrants (in thousands)

Period	Number
1903–1964	22,353
1965–1970	27,757
1971–1980	267,638
1981–1990	333,746
1991–2000	164,166

Source: U.S. Immigration and Naturalization Service.

agreement with Japan in the early 1900s prevented most Japanese immigration to the United States.

Until the 1920s, no numerical restrictions on immigration existed in the United States, although health restrictions applied. The only other significant restrictions came in 1917, when passing a literacy test became a requirement for immigrants. Presidents Cleveland, Taft, and Wilson had vetoed similar measures earlier. In addition, in 1917 a prohibition was added to the law against the immigration of people from Asia (defined as the Asiatic barred zone). While a few of these prohibitions were lifted during World War II, they were not repealed until 1952, and even then Asians were only allowed in under very small annual quotas.

During World War I, the federal government required that all travelers to the United States obtain a visa at a U.S. consulate or diplomatic post abroad. As former State Department consular affairs officer C. D. Scully points out, by making that requirement permanent Congress, by 1924, established the framework of temporary, or non-immigrant visas (for study, work, or travel), and immigrant visas (for permanent residence). That framework remains in place today.

After World War I, cultural intolerance and bizarre racial theories led to new immigration restrictions. The House Judiciary Committee employed a eugenics consultant, Dr. Harry N. Laughlin, who asserted that certain races were inferior. Another leader of the eugenics movement, Madison Grant, argued that Jews, Italians, and others were inferior because of their supposedly different skull size.

Uncle Sam blocks the funnel of immigrants coming to the United States in this political cartoon attacking the Temporary Quota Act of 1921. The 1921 act, along with the Immigration Act of 1924, prevented most southern Europeans, as well as nearly all Asians, from entering the United States.

The Immigration Act of 1924, preceded by the Temporary Quota Act of 1921, set new numerical limits on immigration based on "national origin." Taking effect in 1929, the 1924 act set annual quotas on immigrants that were specifically designed to keep out southern Europeans, such as Italians and Greeks. Generally no more than 100 people of the proscribed nationalities were permitted to immigrate.

While the new law was rigid, the U.S. Department of State's restrictive interpretation directed consular officers overseas to be even stricter in their application of the "public charge" provision. (A public charge is someone unable to support himself or his family.) As author Laura Fermi wrote, "In response to the new cry for restriction at the beginning of the [Great Depression] . . . the consuls were to interpret very strictly the clause prohibiting admission of aliens 'likely to become public charges; and to deny the visa to an applicant who in their opinion might become a public charge at any time.'"

In the early 1900s, more than one million immigrants a year came to the United States. In 1930—the first year of the national-origin quotas—approximately 241,700 immigrants were admitted. But under the State Department's strict interpretations, only 23,068 immigrants entered during 1933, the smallest total since 1831. Later these restrictions prevented many Jews in Germany and elsewhere in Europe from escaping what would become the Holocaust. At the height of the Holocaust in 1943, the United States admitted fewer than 6,000 refugees.

The Displaced Persons Act of 1948, the nation's first refugee law, allowed many refugees from World War II to settle in the United States. The law put into place policy changes that had already seen immigration rise from 38,119 in 1945 to 108,721 in 1946 (and later to 249,187 in 1950). One-third of those admitted between 1948 and 1951 were Poles, with ethnic Germans forming the second-largest group.

The 1952 Immigration and Nationality Act is best known for its restrictions against those who supported communism or anarchy. However, the bill's other provisions were quite restrictive

Upon signing into law the Immigration Act of 1965, President Lyndon B. Johnson declared that the national-origin quota system would "never again shadow the gate to the American nation with the twin barriers of prejudice and privilege." The act removed obstacles to immigration for Koreans and other Asian groups.

and were passed over the veto of President Truman. The 1952 act retained the national-origin quota system for the Eastern Hemisphere. The Western Hemisphere continued to operate without a quota and relied on other qualitative factors to limit immigration. Moreover, during that time, the Mexican bracero program, from 1942 to 1964, allowed millions of Mexican agricultural workers to work temporarily in the United States.

The 1952 act set aside half of each national quota to be divided among three preference categories for relatives of U.S. citizens and permanent residents. The other half went to aliens with high education or exceptional abilities. These quotas applied only to those from the Eastern Hemisphere.

The Immigration and Nationality Act of 1965 became a landmark in immigration legislation by specifically striking the racially based national-origin quotas. It removed the barriers to Asian immigration, which later led to opportunities to immigrate for many Filipinos, Chinese, Koreans, and others. The Western Hemisphere was designated a ceiling of 120,000 immigrants but without a preference system or per country limits.

Modifications made in 1978 ultimately combined the Western and Eastern Hemispheres into one preference system and one ceiling of 290,000.

The 1965 act built on the existing system—without the national-origin quotas—and gave somewhat more priority to family relationships. It did not completely overturn the existing system but rather carried forward essentially intact the family immigration categories from the 1959 amendments to the Immigration and Nationality Act. Even though the text of the law prior to 1965 indicated that half of the immigration slots were reserved for skilled employment immigration, in practice, Immigration and Naturalization Service (INS) statistics show that 86 percent of the visas issued between 1952 and 1965 went for family immigration.

A number of significant pieces of legislation since 1980 have shaped the current U.S. immigration system. First, the Refugee

Flanked by members of Congress, President George W. Bush signs the Enhanced Border Security and Visa Entry Reform Act, May 14, 2002. The legislation, which came in response to the September 11, 2001, terrorist attacks on the United States, tightened rules on the granting of visas.

Act of 1980 removed refugees from the annual world limit and established that the president would set the number of refugees who could be admitted each year after consultations with Congress.

Second, the 1986 Immigration Reform and Control Act (IRCA) introduced sanctions against employers who "knowingly" hired undocumented immigrants (those here illegally). It also provided amnesty for many undocumented immigrants.

Third, the Immigration Act of 1990 increased legal immigration by 40 percent. In particular, the act significantly increased the number of employment-based immigrants (to 140,000), while also boosting family immigration.

Fourth, the 1996 Illegal Immigration Reform and Immigrant Responsibility Act (IIRAIRA) significantly tightened rules that permitted undocumented immigrants to convert to legal status and made other changes that tightened immigration law in areas such as political asylum and deportation.

Fifth, in response to the September 11, 2001, terrorist attacks, the USA PATRIOT Act and the Enhanced Border Security and Visa Entry Reform Act tightened rules on the granting of visas to individuals from certain countries and enhanced the federal government's monitoring and detention authority over foreign nationals in the United States.

In a dramatic reorganization of the federal government, the Homeland Security Act of 2002 abolished the Immigration and Naturalization Service and transferred its immigration service and enforcement functions from the Department of Justice into a new Department of Homeland Security. The Customs Service, the Coast Guard, and parts of other agencies were also transferred into the new department.

The Department of Homeland Security, with regards to immigration, is organized as follows: The Bureau of Customs and Border Protection (BCBP) contains Customs and Immigration inspectors, who check the documents of travelers to the United States at air, sea, and land ports of entry; and Border Patrol agents, the uniformed agents who seek to prevent unlawful entry along the southern and northern border. The new Bureau of Immigration and Customs Enforcement (BICE) employs investigators, who attempt to find undocumented immigrants inside the United States, and Detention and Removal officers, who detain and seek to deport such individuals. The new

Electing to Stay

Lawful permanent residents may, but are not required to, seek American citizenship—a process that is called naturalization. To be naturalized, the person must live in the United States for at least five years (unless he or she is married to an American citizen, in which case the minimum is three years) and pass a citizenship exam. Children of applicants usually become naturalized along with their parents.

The decision to naturalize is not an easy one: in return for American citizenship, the person gives up citizenship in his or her country of origin. For many, however, perceived anti-immigrant sentiment in the United States during the 1990s tipped the balance in favor of citizenship. "Many have become citizens as soon as they have become eligible, and others who earlier chose not to renounce the citizenship of their birth have recently taken this step," writes Uma A. Segal.

When Miyong T. Kim and her husband came to the United States, it was so he could earn a Ph.D. in sociology at the University of Arizona. "The plan was that after [he] completed his studies, we'd go back to Korea," says Kim, who trained as a nurse in her homeland. "I started working and taking classes, and soon I fell in love with the cultural experiences and diversity of ideas that could be found in America."

Ultimately, both Kim and her husband earned doctorates (hers is in nursing research) and moved to Baltimore, Maryland, with their two sons. Kim, who left South Korea at 27, agonized over the decision to stay in the United States. "I was attached to my family, and in a way, I felt as though I was divorcing my country," she says.

It was the voting booth that finally swayed Kim, today a professor and researcher at the Johns Hopkins School of Nursing, to seek American citizenship. Kim came from a family that encouraged intellectual and political discussion. "It was difficult for me to be in the United States and not be able to vote on Election Day," she says. Since 1996, when Kim took the oath of citizenship, she has been exercising one of the most fundamental and treasured privileges of being an American.

U.S. Department of State

APPLICATION FOR IMMIGRANT VISA AND ALIEN REGISTRATION

OMB APPROVAL NO. 1405-0015
EXPIRES: 05/31/2004
ESTIMATED BURDEN: 1 HOUR*
(See Page 2)

PART I - BIOGRAPHIC DATA

INSTRUCTIONS: Complete one copy of this form for yourself and each member of your family, regardless of age, who will immigrate with you. Please print or type your answers to all questions. Mark questions that are Not Applicable with "N/A". If there is insufficient room on the form, answer on a separate sheet using the same numbers that appear on the form. Attach any additional sheets to this form.

WARNING: Any false statement or concealment of a material fact may result in your permanent exclusion from the United States.

This form (DS-230 PART I) is the first of two parts. This part, together with Form DS-230 PART II, constitutes the complete Application for Immigrant Visa and Alien Registration.

1. Family Name | First Name | Middle Name

2. Other Names Used or Aliases (If married woman, give maiden name)

3. Full Name in Native Alphabet (If Roman letters not used)

4. Date of Birth (mm-dd-yyyy) | 5. Age | 6. Place of Birth (City or town) (Province) (Country)

7. Nationality (If dual national, give both) | 8. Gender ☐ Male ☐ Female | 9. Marital Status ☐ Single (Never married) ☐ Married ☐ Widowed ☐ Divorced ☐ Separated
Including my present marriage, I have been married _____ times.

10. Permanent address in the United States where you intend to live, if known (street address including zip code). Include the name of a person who currently lives there.

11. Address in the United States where you want your Permanent Resident Card (Green Card) mailed, if different from address in item #10 (include the name of a person who currently lives there).

Telephone number: | Telephone number:

12. Your Present Occupation | 13. Present Address (Street Address) (City or Town) (Province) (Country)

Telephone number: Home | Office

14. Name of Spouse (Maiden or family name) | First Name | Middle Name

Date (mm-dd-yyyy) and place of birth of spouse:

Address of spouse (If different from your own):

Spouse's occupation: | Date of marriage (mm-dd-yyyy):

15. Father's Family Name | First Name | Middle Name

16. Father's Date of Birth (mm-dd-yyyy) | Place of Birth | Current Address | If deceased, give year of death

17. Mother's Family Name at Birth | First Name | Middle Name

18. Mother's Date of Birth (mm-dd-yyyy) | Place of Birth | Current Address | If deceased, give year of death

DS-230 Part I
05-2001

THIS FORM MAY BE OBTAINED FREE AT CONSULAR OFFICES OF THE UNITED STATES OF AMERICA
PREVIOUS EDITIONS OBSOLETE

Page 1 of 4

Bureau of Citizenship and Immigration Services (BCIS) is where people go, or correspond with, to become U.S. citizens or obtain permission to work or extend their stay in the United States.

Following the terrorist attacks of September 11, 2001, the Department of Justice adopted several measures that did not require new legislation to be passed by Congress. Some of these measures created controversy and raised concerns about civil liberties. For example, FBI and INS agents detained for months more than 1,000 foreign nationals of Middle Eastern descent and refused to release the names of the individuals. It is alleged that the Department of Justice adopted tactics that discouraged the detainees from obtaining legal assistance. The Department of Justice also began requiring foreign nationals from primarily Muslim nations to be fingerprinted and questioned by immigration officers upon entry or if they have been living in the United States. Those involved in the September 11 attacks were not immigrants—people who become permanent residents with a right to stay in the United States—but holders of temporary visas, primarily visitor or tourist visas.

Today, the annual rate of legal immigration is lower than that at earlier periods in U.S. history. For example, from 1901 to 1910 approximately 10.4 immigrants per 1,000 U.S. residents came to the United States. Today, the annual rate is about 3.5 immigrants per 1,000 U.S. residents. While the percentage of foreign-born people in the U.S. population has risen above 11 percent, it remains lower than the 13 percent or higher that prevailed in the country from 1860 to 1930. Still, as has been the case previously in U.S. history, some people argue that even legal immigration should be lowered. These people maintain that immigrants take jobs native-born Americans could fill and that U.S. population growth, which immigration contributes to, harms the environment. In 1996 Congress voted against efforts to reduce legal immigration.

Most immigrants (800,000 to one million annually) enter the United States legally. But over the years the undocumented (illegal) portion of the population has increased to about 2.8 percent of the U.S. population—approximately 8 million people in all.

Today, the legal immigration system in the United States contains many rules, permitting only individuals who fit into certain categories to immigrate—and in many cases only after waiting anywhere from 1 to 10 years or more. The system, representing a compromise among family, employment, and human rights concerns, has the following elements:

A U.S. citizen may sponsor for immigration a spouse, parent, sibling, or minor or adult child.

A lawful permanent resident (green card holder) may sponsor only a spouse or child.

A foreign national may immigrate if he or she gains an employer sponsor.

An individual who can show that he or she has a "well-founded fear of persecution" may come to the country as a refugee—or be allowed to stay as an asylee (someone who receives asylum).

San Francisco is home to more than 7,600 Korean Americans, according to the 2000 census. The Bay City's Korean American community dates to the World War I era, when about 1,000 Korean immigrants moved from Hawaii to the West Coast.

Beyond these categories, essentially the only other way to immigrate is to apply for and receive one of the "diversity" visas, which are granted annually by lottery to those from "underrepresented" countries.

In 1996 changes to the law prohibited nearly all incoming immigrants from being eligible for federal public benefits, such as welfare, during their first five years in the country. Refugees were mostly excluded from these changes. In addition, families who sponsor relatives must sign an affidavit of support showing they can financially take care of an immigrant who falls on hard times.

The First Wave of Korean Immigration

A few Koreans came to America in the late 1800s, but it wasn't until 1903 that Korean immigration began in earnest. The Hawaiian Sugar Planters' Association needed people to work on the sugar plantations, and Korean workers, mostly men, were brought over as a source of cheap labor. The Koreans earned about $1 a day, and they paid the sugar company $1 a month to cover the cost of their passage from Korea to Hawaii. Later that year, a San Francisco man, S. F. Moore, concerned over reports that the Korean workers were being mistreated, went to Hawaii to see for himself. As he was relieved to report,

> We found that each Korean family is given a house, or some-times two families occupy one house having rooms separate. The houses are small and are nicely located on high ground. They are kept white with whitewash and were clean.

> Each man is given his fuel and a patch of ground to raise his vegetables; water is also supplied for irrigating their gardens. Medicine and a doctor's services are also provided by the company. A school is provided for the children where there are any to attend it, and also a room used for school at night and for church on Sunday. The night school is taught by a Korean who knows some English.

By 1905 a total of 7,226 Koreans had left the peninsula for the tropical sugar fields.

In 2003 Americans and Koreans alike celebrated the centennial of Korean immigration to the United States with festivals, concerts, and museum exhibits. On January 13, 2003, the 100th anniversary of the arrival of the first Korean workers in Honolulu, President George W. Bush issued a proclamation, which read in part:

> As we commemorate the centennial anniversary of Korean immigration to the United States, we recognize the invaluable contributions of Korean Americans to our Nation's rich cultural diversity, economic strength, and proud heritage.

> For the past century, Korean immigrants and their descendants have helped build America's prosperity, strengthened America's communities, and defended America's freedoms. Through their service in World War I, World War II, the Korean Conflict, the

Vietnam War, and other wars, Korean Americans have served our Nation with honor and courage, upholding the values that make our country strong.

As World War I (1914–1918) unfolded, some plantation workers left Hawaii for the U.S. mainland. San Francisco became a center of the Korean American community.

With Japan's occupation of Korea and restrictive U.S. immigration laws passed in 1917 and 1924, very few Koreans left the peninsula and fewer still were able to enter America. One exception was the "picture brides," women whose photographs were sent to Korean bachelors for the purpose of arranging marriages.

The Second Wave

Brides played an important role in the second wave of Korean immigration to the United States. The War Brides Act of 1945 exempted foreign wives and children of American servicemen from immigration quotas, enabling families to be reunited. Still, Korean women didn't come to the United States in high numbers until after the Korean War. In fact, only one Korean woman came to the United States as an American citizen's wife in 1952; by 1964, though, 1,339 more spouses arrived. Korean orphans adopted by Americans also came during this wave; many were children with white fathers.

The Third Wave

The third wave of Korean immigration began with President Lyndon Johnson's signing of the Immigration Act of 1965. Many Koreans accepted the opportunity to come to America, whether to reunite with families, study, or pursue the American Dream. In the years 1965–1970, the United States welcomed a total of 27,757 legal Korean immigrants. The numbers rose dramatically between 1971 and 1980, with 267,638 newcomers from the Korean Peninsula. The United States received 333,746 Korean immigrants between 1981 and 1990, with the third wave of Korean immigration reaching its crest in 1987, at

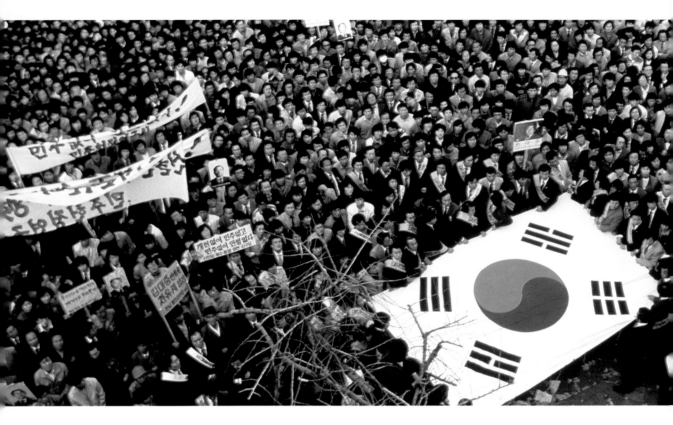

35,849. Thereafter, Korean immigration to the United States declined somewhat. In all, 164,166 Koreans made the United States their new home in the 1991–2000 period. Korean immigration figures for 2001 and 2002 were 20,742 and 21,021, respectively.

Slowdowns in INS processing inside the country may be a key reason for much of the change in the annual number of Korean immigrants to the United States. In the mid-1990s, the Immigration and Naturalization Service began to focus its resources on the burgeoning backlog of naturalization applications. That focus created a large backlog for permanent residence cases, those involving individuals already inside the country in legal status (such as a temporary worker applying for a green card with an employer). As the INS increased the processing of permanent residence cases, immigration numbers changed. In the case of Koreans, the numbers rose from 12,840 in 1999 to 21,021 in 2002.

A huge crowd displays banners and the South Korean flag during the 1988 Summer Olympics. The Seoul Games showcased a nation that had emerged from conflict and poverty as a prosperous and progressive society.

U.S. waiting lists to immigrate may be another factor. In family categories that Korean immigrants would use—siblings and adult children of U.S. citizens and spouses of lawful permanent residents (green card holders)—significant waiting lists have existed that may have slowed Korean immigration. The waiting time for a U.S. citizen to sponsor a brother or sister from Korea is more than 10 years.

Until the late 1990s, South Korea was in the midst of an economic boom, which may have encouraged some people to stay home rather than emigrate or come to school in the United States. One of the so-called Four Asian Tigers (along with Taiwan, Hong Kong, and Singapore), South Korea experienced economic growth rates that, particularly from the late 1970s on, outstripped those of the industrialized West. Socially, South Korea appeared to be making great strides as well. The 1988 Summer Olympics, hosted by Seoul, were a source of pride for South Koreans and showcased their thriving country to the world. The theme—"Peace, Harmony, Progress"—seemed an apt description of the nation as a whole, and among those who took notice were Koreans who had emigrated.

On the 2000 U.S. census, more than 12 percent of Korean American respondents listed their ancestry as "Asian in combination with one or more races." The trend toward intermarriage marks a significant difference between the Korean American community and Koreans on the racially homogeneous peninsula.

A Demographic Snapshot
of Korean Americans

Three categories of Korean American immigrants are
described by Moon Jo in *Korean Immigrants and the Challenge
of Adjustment*: those who want to remain in the United States
no matter how good the situation is in Korea; those who
intend to make a living in the United States but retire in Korea;
and those who are unhappy in the United States and wish to go
back to the Korean Peninsula.

The 2000 U.S. census reports that there are more than 1.1
million Koreans living in the United States. Korean Americans
are the fifth-largest group of Asian Americans and live in every
state. The five states with the largest Korean populations are:

In recent years
Canada has become
an increasingly pop-
ular destination for
Korean immigrants.

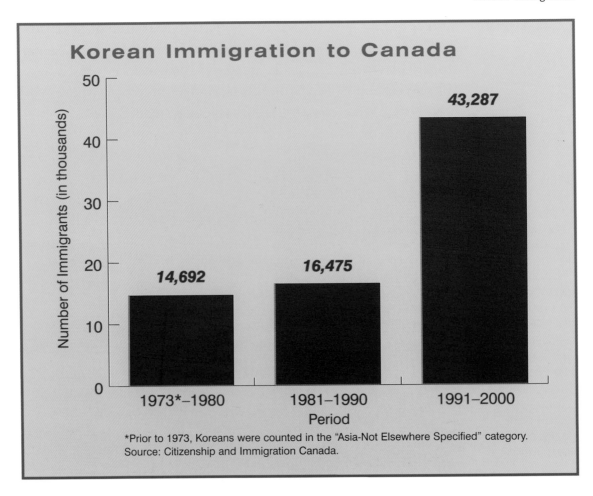

Korean Immigration to Canada

Number of Immigrants (in thousands)

- 1973*–1980: 14,692
- 1981–1990: 16,475
- 1991–2000: 43,287

Period

*Prior to 1973, Koreans were counted in the "Asia-Not Elsewhere Specified" category.
Source: Citizenship and Immigration Canada.

California, 345,882; New York, 119,846; New Jersey, 65,349; Illinois, 51,453; and Washington, 46,880. By contrast, the census of 2000 recorded only 857 Koreans residing in West Virginia.

Boston, Massachusetts, is one of the boom areas for Korean Americans, according to the 2000 census. Koreans are the third-fastest-growing ethnic group in the city known as "Beantown," trailing two other Asian nationalities, Vietnamese and Asian Indians. In 1990 there were 1,146 Koreans living in Boston; 10 years later, their numbers had swelled to 2,564, a 123 percent increase. Meanwhile, Boston's white population declined 11 percent.

Traditionally, Koreans have settled in large cities such as Los Angeles and New York. Koreans are New York City's third-largest Asian community, and their numbers increased 24 percent, to 86,473, between 1990 and 2000. But the 2000 census also showed dramatic growth in smaller enclaves—the Korean American population of Washington State, for example, grew 58 percent between 1990 and 2000.

In 2000, for the first time, the census allowed people to identify themselves as being from more than one race. In the past, for instance, a person who had one white parent and one Korean parent had to decide which ethnicity to identify with, white or Asian. In the 2000 count, 10.2 million people identified themselves as "Asian alone," but another 1.7 million said they were "Asian alone or in combination." Among Korean Americans who completed the census, 1,076,872 described themselves as "Asian alone," but another 129,000, or about 12.3 percent of all Korean respondents, chose "Asian in combination with one or more races." That means that Korean Americans are marrying and having children with people from other racial and ethnic backgrounds, a trend that would be unlikely to develop in their racially homogeneous homeland.

Virtually all Koreans who immigrate to the United States today are from South Korea. In 2003, under a State Department–administered program that annually awards, through a lottery, 50,000 permanent residence visas to applicants from countries with low migration rates to the United States, just 4 North Koreans became eligible for visas. The previous year, the United States granted asylum status to a North Korean for the first time (most North Koreans seeking asylum settle in South Korea). The man, and another North Korean who also applied for asylum, were attempting to cross the Mexican-U.S. border when American authorities apprehended them. The men said they were defectors and requested political asylum.

Canada: An Increasingly Popular Destination

Canada, which actively promotes immigration, is becoming the new home for a growing number of Koreans. In the 1996 Canadian census, some 66,650 people said they were of Korean descent. During the years 1991–2000 alone, 43,287 Koreans immigrated to Canada. Korea was the fifth-highest source country of immigrants to Canada in 1999 and 2000.

It wasn't always that way. As in the United States, Canadian immigration policy has broadened in recent decades. A 1910 law gave European immigrants preference and charged a "head tax" on those of Asian descent. Although a 1962 law eliminated racial qualifiers, it specified that newcomers to Canada must have a job waiting for them or be able to support themselves financially. Then, in response to a report touting the benefits of immigration—including economic growth—and for other reasons, Canada implemented a points system in 1967. This system awards points to potential immigrants based on their skills and Canada's economic needs. The 1976 Canadian Immigration Act created five categories of immigrants and allowed for family reunification.

What attracts Koreans to Canada? Although 75 percent of Korean immigrants enter the country as skilled workers, the Canadian educational system is also a strong draw. According to the Canadian embassy in Seoul, 11,000 student visas were issued in 2000 to Koreans pursuing an education in Canada, and applications that year were up 300 percent over 1998.

Canada's government has made clear its desire for immigrants—"new" Canadians who will fill voids left by the country's aging population. Indeed, without immigration, Canada would soon face a demographic crisis. In 2002 Citizenship and Immigration Canada—the agency responsible for overseeing immigration into the country—predicted that within a decade, newcomers will account for all of the growth in Canada's labor force. And by 2026, Canada's population is expected to grow only through immigration. Because of the vital role that immigrants will play in Canada's future, the country extends a hand of friendship to newcomers. The government encourages its citizens to volunteer in the Host Program, which matches immigrants with Canadians who show them around a community, help them become familiar with local businesses and schools, and introduce them to Canadian culture. Even municipal officials see the benefits of immigration. In 2002, for example, Winnipeg became part of a pilot program to assist refugees, which, its sponsors hoped, would help the city "get its fair share of new Canadians."

4 A New Land, A New Life

Moving to a new country presents many challenges. Among the most immediate questions immigrants face are where to live and how to support themselves. Frequently, adjusting to life in the new country is made even more difficult by unfamiliarity with its language, customs, and culture.

Family Matters

For Koreans—whether in their homeland or on foreign soil—family is a constant. Korean culture places great importance on family relations. Parents make sacrifices for their children, especially in the name of education. Children, in turn, generally accept responsibility to care for their mothers and fathers when they become elderly.

Where immigration is concerned, family members take on a new significance: Koreans already living in the United States can act as "sponsors" for their relatives. It is common for a young adult member of a Korean family to come to America first, then bring over other relatives. However, given backlogs and waiting lists it can sometimes take 10 years or more, depending on the immigration category, to sponsor a relative to the United States.

Like other new immigrants, many Koreans are drawn to neighborhoods where others originally from their homeland live. Korean neighborhoods in large cities such as New York,

◄ Beginnings: Happy Korean immigrants upon arrival at an airport in their new land. In 2001 Canada recorded more than 9,600 new Korean immigrants; the United States, more than 20,700 Korean newcomers.

Los Angeles, and Toronto are known as Koreatowns—ethnic enclaves that function primarily as business centers and social hubs for the Korean people. There conversations are conducted in the Korean language, which also appears on street signs and storefront windows.

New York City actually has two major centers of Korean activity. Many Korean Americans live in Flushing, Queens, which has a host of Korean businesses to serve them. And in midtown Manhattan, at Broadway and 27th to 32nd Streets, is the area known as the Korean Trading Avenue.

In Los Angeles, Koreatown is not only an ethnic enclave with Korean bookstores, clothing stores, restaurants, and nightclubs, but also a tourist attraction. The demographics of L.A.'s Koreatown have changed over the years; now, many Latinos live there. In response to this ethnic shift, the Korean Youth and Community Center offers programs and services for Latino as well as Korean youth.

Although many Korean immigrants gravitate toward urban centers, many others make their homes in smaller towns and suburbs. Palisades Park, New Jersey, is a town to which new Italian and Irish immigrants flocked at the beginning of the 20th century. One hundred years later, Koreans account for more than 40 percent of the town's population of 15,050. And

A Los Angeles street sign. Thriving Korean communities also exist in other major North American cities, such as New York and Toronto, as well as in smaller suburban areas like Palisades Park, New Jersey.

Palisades Park's Korean community has grown quickly. According to the U.S. Census Bureau, the number of Koreans living in the Bergen County town soared from 1,661 to 6,065 between 1990 and 2000—an increase of 265 percent. A computer-store owner, quoted in the *Bergen Record* newspaper, said, "Not many years ago, a lot of Koreans didn't know Broad Avenue existed. There were just a few Koreans, not many. Now Koreans all over . . . know that Broad Avenue is where you can find anything Korean that you need."

The Church

After family, the most important institution to many Korean immigrants is the Christian church. The Catholic faith was introduced to Koreans in the 17th century, and Protestant missionaries arrived on the Korean Peninsula in the late 1800s. Today in Korea, a traditionally Buddhist country, about half of the population has embraced Christianity.

The percentage of Christians dramatically increases among Korean immigrants. About 70 percent of Korean Americans are church members, and many of them regularly attend services, notes R. Stephen Warner in the book *Korean Americans and Their Religions: Pilgrims and Missionaries from a Different Shore*. Of those Korean Americans who profess the Christian faith, most are Protestants rather than Catholics.

Christians are more likely to emigrate from Korea than their countrymen and women who have other religious beliefs, and they are also considered "modernizers" who are interested in improving their lives. Most Korean churches in North America are separate congregations with ties to major denominations such as Methodists and Presbyterians. In comparison, only about 5 percent of Korean Americans practice Buddhism, with Buddhist priests in the United States taking on more of a missionary role, seeking American converts to their faith. Ironically, the Unification Church, which was introduced to the United States by the Reverend Sun Myung Moon in the 1960s, has relatively few followers in Moon's home country, Korea, or

even among Koreans in the United States.

For Korean immigrants, the Christian church serves many purposes, as the editors of *East to America: Korean American Life Stories* explain: "In the Korean American community, no other organizations can match the Christian church in terms of size, influence, and financial resources. For many Koreans, church is the principal place for making friends, forming support networks, and exchanging information about jobs, business opportunities, social service programs, and schooling for children."

The Korean Presbyterian Church of Elizabeth, New Jersey, like many Korean American congregations, has two services: one conducted in Korean, the other in English. After Sunday worship, everyone is invited to a lunch. Church members take turns preparing traditional Korean food for about 300 people. The Reverend Isaac Ahn, the church's associate pastor, says that to some congregants, the cultural and social elements of a

The Reverend Sun Myung Moon and his wife preside over a mass-wedding ceremony of Unification Church members at Madison Square Garden in New York City, 1982. Moon's religion, founded in the 1960s, has attracted very few followers in his native South Korea or in the Korean immigrant communities of North America.

Korean church have been more important than the spiritual elements. "Especially during the 1970s and 1980s, the Koreans coming to the United States couldn't function well in American society. They didn't know English, or they operated small businesses in bad neighborhoods," says Ahn. "Korean church was a haven to them because they could speak the language, function well in the culture, and have a voice in the running of the church."

While the church has been a tremendous source of support for first-generation Korean Americans and Canadians, there are indications that it will not have the same significance for future generations. One pastor, Min Ho Song, conducted a study of 300 second-generation Korean Canadians. He found that one-third were active churchgoers, one-third described themselves as "marginal" Christians, and one-third no longer attended church. The second generation's ambivalence toward

Yearn Hong Choi, a poet and university professor, immigrated to the United States in 1968. His poem "My Sail" explores his feelings about leaving one country for another.

My Sail

A gull

And solitude with the solidity of a thing.

My sail shines fresh venturing alone

In the shadow of the Pacific.

What am I searching for in a distant land?

What have I cast off in my native land?

The waves are playing, the winds whistle,

And the mast bows and creaks.

Alas! I am searching for happiness!

Below the soul a stream of glistening azure,

Between the vast expanse of the sky

And the waters.

church could be their response to the "cultural rigidity" of the first generation, or it may simply reflect the fact that their parents didn't emphasize spiritual matters at home, suggests Song.

After family and the church, college or work-related associations provide the most important support mechanisms for Korean immigrants. Many younger Koreans come to the United States or Canada to study, and there are Korean or Asian student organizations on virtually every major college campus. Once the students graduate, Korean or Asian alumni associations offer networking and social opportunities. Many Korean immigrants operate small businesses and rely on industry-specific associations for support.

Koreans in the Workplace

The Korean people place a high value on education, and most adult Korean immigrants have college degrees or have completed some higher education. According to Dr. Hang Yul Rhee, president of the International Council on Korean Studies, there are about 2,000 professors of Korean descent working at North American colleges; thousands more are employed in professional fields, such as medicine and engineering.

Those numbers are impressive, but many Koreans do not work in their chosen fields once in America. One survey of Korean female immigrants revealed that 68 percent of the respondents' husbands had blue-collar (manual or industrial) jobs in America, but 54 percent had held white-collar (professional) jobs in Korea. If professional credentials do not transfer easily to the United States or Canada or the person does not speak English well, high-level, professional jobs might be out of reach—at least temporarily, but sometimes permanently. The Korean American grocer, dry cleaner, or nail-salon owner might have impressive academic credentials or a solid résumé.

In *Korean Immigrants and the Challenge of Adjustment*, Moon Jo tells what one Korean American did with his master of business administration degree: "[He] decided to open a bakery in a suburb of Washington. He viewed his chances for success in an American firm as rather slim because of his limited command of English and racism. He figured that, instead of wasting his time working for an American firm, he ought to start his own business."

Korean rates of entrepreneurship appear to be the highest of any immigrant group in America. U.S. Census figures report that as many as 25 percent of Korean immigrants over 25 years old are self-employed, meaning they work for themselves in their own business. This means that Korean immigrants are more than twice as likely as native-born Americans to be self-employed.

Korean Americans own 135,571 businesses, yielding gross

North American colleges and universities employ an estimated 2,000 people of Korean descent as professors, according to the International Council on Korean Studies. In addition, thousands of Korean immigrants work in technical and professional fields. But many highly educated first-generation Korean Americans and Korean Canadians hold blue-collar jobs or operate small businesses such as dry cleaners and grocery stores.

How to Succeed in Business

As a recruitment specialist who understands the business world, Jino Ahn was struck by how many of the highly touted corporate diversity programs were incomplete. "African Americans and Latinos were making progress, but Asian Americans were left out," he says. In response, Ahn founded Asian Diversity, Inc., a New York–based organization that sponsors job fairs, offers career search and recruitment services, publishes an online magazine, and provides training to human resources personnel, all with the goal of empowering Asians in the workplace.

Asian stereotypes—both positive and negative—abound in the workplace. "The good ones are that Asians are good with numbers and hard workers. On the other hand, we're also viewed as quiet and submissive—not leadership material," notes Ahn, who immigrated to the United States from South Korea when he was a teenager. "While being reserved is considered a virtue to Asians, we need to hold true to our value system yet learn to adapt to the positive aspects of the American workplace."

Ahn believes Asians are making progress in the corporate world, particularly in the information technology and financial sectors. "But change isn't going to happen overnight," he says. "We have to keep working on it."

sales of $46 billion, according to the 2000 U.S. census. About 20 percent of all dry cleaning businesses in the United States are run by Korean Americans, who are also the proprietors of 45 percent of the one-hour photo shops and 45 percent of the liquor stores in Southern California. Usually, newly arrived Koreans learn a business by working for family members or friends, with the dream of having their own store someday.

It takes a fair amount of money to open or buy a business. For many years, the Korean government had strict limits on how much money an emigrant could take out of the country—as little as $1,000 in 1978. And banks might not be willing to write a loan to a newly arrived immigrant. So how have Koreans amassed the capital to start their businesses? Kyeyoung Park wrote about Korean small-business owners from Queens, New York, in her book *The Korean American Dream: Immigrants and Small Business in New York City*. She found that they used savings, personal loans, money they had brought from Korea, and gifts; only a small proportion (2 percent) took out a bank loan. About 4 in 10 of the business owners also participated in rotating credit clubs known as *kyes*. Members of a *kye* contribute money to a pool on a regular basis, with participants taking turns to receive the lump sum. Like the Korean American church, the *kye* can take on a significance beyond its original purpose. It can also play a social role, helping immigrants establish friendships in their new country. "I suspect that, among those financially secure Koreans who use rotating credit clubs for business investment, their use still will persist even when they have a greater familiarity with the American banking system," notes Park. *Kyes* are less utilized among second-generation Korean Americans, who use more traditional sources of financing. The Korean government now also permits emigrants to take as much as $200,000 with them when they leave the country.

The Koreans' success at small business has not come without a cost. Many of the stores are located in run-down neighborhoods, and relations between store owners and customers have sometimes been tense. The employees and owner of a store often work many hours. Although the owner might take a personal interest in a Korean employee, the pay is typically low and the work constant. "When work tasks are completed at the typical Korean workplace, employees are not supposed to rest, sit down, or read a newspaper," notes Park. From the store owners' perspective, hiring fellow Koreans doesn't always work out that well, either. In a survey of nearly 1,000 Korean store owners, Korean employees were described as temporary workers who would quickly ask for a pay raise, then abruptly quit if the request were turned down. Korean store owners also sometimes have a poor understanding of American tax and labor laws (neglecting to deduct federal taxes from paychecks, for instance). However, Moon Jo believes it is too early to pronounce judgment on Korean American businesspeople. "Korean entrepreneurs are still learning to run small-sized or medium-sized businesses, overcoming language and cultural barriers and racial prejudice," he says.

A Helping Hand

Family, church, and employment form the frame of a new life in the United States or Canada for recently arrived Korean immigrants. But other organizations serve as gathering places or sources of information for newcomers.

In Toronto, for example, the YMCA Korean Program can help in the search for housing or a job, assist with filling out governmental forms, and provide translation and interpreting

California, New York, and New Jersey are the top states for new Korean Americans.

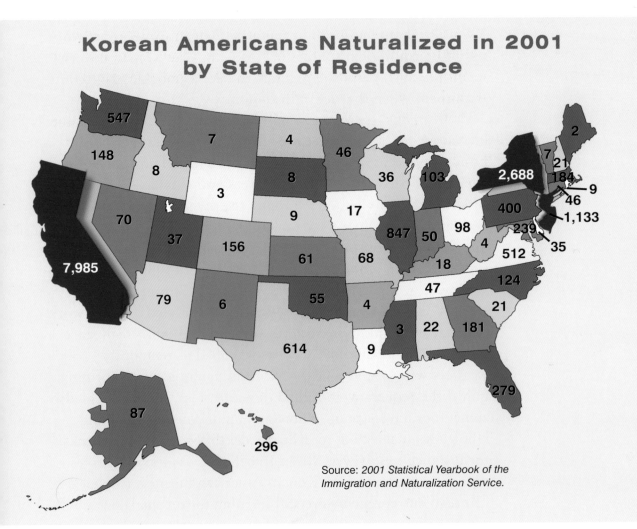

Korean Americans Naturalized in 2001 by State of Residence

547
148
8
7
4
46
2
7
21
184
36
103
2,688
9
3
8
9
17
400
46
70
847
50
98
239
1,133
37
156
4
35
7,985
61
68
18
512
79
6
55
4
47
124
3
22
181
21
614
9
279
87
296

Source: *2001 Statistical Yearbook of the Immigration and Naturalization Service.*

services. The YMCA also offers a children's program, a citizenship class, and a knitting club for senior Koreans.

Major cities throughout North America have Korean associations or chambers of commerce that can provide assistance and social outlets. Some are concerned with empowering the Korean American community (helping newly naturalized citizens register to vote, for example). Others have a cultural focus. And many times, the groups are a blend of both. The Young Korean American Service & Education Center, based in New York City, sponsors an immigrants' rights project, has a cultural troupe that participates in Lunar New Year festivals and other traditional Korean activities, and offers classes in traditional Korean drumming.

Starting over in a new country is never an easy task. But pioneer Korean immigrants have laid the groundwork for their countrymen and women to come to the United States and Canada.

"For the many newly arrived Koreans, the social support offered by their compatriots is sometimes as important as economic survival," writes Moon Jo. "Establishing a connection with members of the Korean community is quite easy. All one has to do is reach out to other Koreans at churches, at sporting events, at picnics, and at many other Korean community-sponsored functions."

5 A PART OF NORTH AMERICAN SOCIETY, OR APART FROM IT?

The Korean sugar plantation workers who arrived in Hawaii in 1903 initially expected to return to the peninsula. But since 1965, coming to America or Canada is a choice that many, though not all, Koreans intend to be a permanent one. In becoming part of a new society with a vastly different culture, Koreans must decide which values and traditions to keep and which ones to leave behind. These are highly individualized choices, yet they are shaped largely by which generation—first, 1.5, or second—the Korean immigrant represents.

When discussing the lives of immigrants, sociologists and anthropologists frequently refer to the process of assimilation. It's a complex concept, but in the simplest terms, assimilation is when a person from one culture takes on the mind-set, habits, and customs of another culture.

Among the first changes for Korean immigrants is something very personal: their name. In Korea, the person's family name comes first; the Westernized version places the family name second. For instance, in Korea, the founder of the Hyundai Group is Chung Ju-yung. In the United States or Canada, he is known as Ju-yung Chung.

The Language Barrier

Not only do the names change, but so does the dominant language. Fluency in English certainly isn't a problem for

◀ Korean immigrants, like other recent arrivals, tend to adopt certain North American customs while retaining many aspects of their homeland's culture. For the first and 1.5 generations particularly, language can be a major barrier to overcome. Pictured here: a scene from Koreatown in Los Angeles.

second-generation Korean Americans. Members of the 1.5 generation—who typically have learned some English in their Korean school or are enrolled in English as a Second Language class in their new country—also usually do quite well. However, language is a major barrier for some first-generation Korean Americans. According to the U.S. census of 1990, about 40 percent of Korean Americans were described as being "linguistically isolated," and in the 2000 U.S. census, 88 percent of the Korean respondents said they spoke Korean at home.

The Korean language is unlike the English language, with a different alphabet and rules of grammar. For example, in English, sentences usually follow the grammatical pattern of subject, verb, and object—Joe reads books. In Korean grammar, the action word comes at the end of the sentence—Joe books reads. Even if a Korean knows what the English words mean, she might be unable to use correct grammar or be embarrassed by her pronunciation.

Learning the Language

While language may be a barrier for older, first-generation Korean Americans, children born in the United States or arriving here at school age have demonstrated a remarkable ability to learn English, regardless of their country of origin. It is much easier for children to learn a new language than it is for adults.

English as a Second Language (ESL) classes help many school-age immigrant children learn the dominant tongue of their new country. Urban centers with large foreign-born populations have finely tuned ESL programs, but as non-native speakers of English migrate to less populated areas, suburban and rural school districts may have to enhance or even create ESL programs for a handful of students. Some teachers have to learn as they go and make adaptations accordingly. In one Iowa high school, the ESL teacher had two students, Korean brothers. When one of the boys told her he couldn't understand anything written on the blackboard, she realized she had been writing in print letters on the board, while most of the school's teachers wrote in cursive.

In America, linguistic isolation can lead to social isolation and dependency. Job possibilities become more limited; the choices of where to shop, dine, bank, and do many everyday activities can become restricted to the Korean community. Some elderly Korean Americans who speak only Korean are not able to communicate with their second-generation Korean American grandchildren, who speak only English. Parents who aren't fluent in English sometimes depend on their children to translate for them, which reverses the parent-child relationship.

Moon Jo, in his book *Korean Immigrants and the Challenge of Adjustment*, relates the frustration a language barrier can create within the Korean family. One businessman said, "After living in the United States for more than 25 years, my wife is not Americanized at all. She watches Korean videos, listens to Korean news [on a special channel], reads Korean novels, loves Korean food, and even furnishes our house with Korean furniture. Her problem is that I am much more inclined to embrace American culture. Sometimes I feel we don't have much of anything in common to talk about."

The language barrier not only has social and familial implications, but it can also have life-threatening consequences. Dr. Miyong T. Kim, a first-generation Korean American and a professor at the Johns Hopkins School of Nursing, has been working with elderly Korean Americans in the Baltimore area for many years. Most of the seniors she comes across can't speak English fluently enough to communicate well with their doctors. "From a cultural standpoint, if a Korean American senior citizen disagrees with her doctor about treatment, most likely she'll nod her head as if to say, 'You're the doctor—you know best,'" says Kim. In one of Kim's studies of first-generation Korean Americans, she found that many of the respondents needed help from an interpreter to make a doctor's appointment.

Kim says that this underserved population—elderly, first-generation Korean Americans—has many strikes against it. Older people typically have more health-care needs than younger people, and Korean Americans are at high risk for developing type II diabetes, high blood pressure, and hepatitis B. Few older Korean Americans have private health insurance, and many are unaware that they could qualify for Medicaid or Medicare.

Miyong T. Kim and her husband, Kim Kim, have been at the forefront of efforts in the Baltimore area to provide "culturally appropriate" medical care for Korean Americans. Through her academic work at the Johns Hopkins School of Nursing, she's developed programs that use bilingual case managers and bilingual nurses to monitor elderly Korean Americans. Certain patients receive a special in-home blood pressure monitoring device that enables them to transmit the data over the phone. The Korean Resource Center, a nonprofit organization started by Kim Kim, works with Korean nurses, doctors, and dentists to reach out to the community.

"One of my goals is to help Korean Americans become more comfortable—and assertive—with the doctors," says Miyong Kim. "I tell them, 'You are the consumer. The physician is here to serve you.'"

As for social isolation, some within the Korean American community suggest it's time for Koreans to reach out to mainstream society. "We should take every opportunity or create opportunities to get acquainted with our white and black neighbors and hang out with them," wrote novelist Ty Pak in the *Korean Quarterly* newspaper. "We shouldn't miss community events like bazaars, cookouts, raffles, picnics, sports, and games. When there are national or local disasters . . . we should be among the first out there with the rescue workers, conspicuously participating in rallies and prayer vigils, and donating blood and money. We should impress on mainstream America that we are a giving people, reaching out beyond our racial boundary."

Contributions to a New Land

Unquestionably, Korean immigrants have made important and lasting contributions to their new country. Many have become American success stories and even household names.

Although Jhoon Rhee was not part of the post-1965 group of Korean immigrants to the United States (he arrived in 1957), this world-renowned master of Tae Kwon Do introduced the Korean martial art to countless Americans. Quite fittingly, he is known as "the Father of American Tae Kwon Do." Rhee served as an adviser to the Presidential Council on Physical Fitness & Sports during the 1980s, has taught Tae Kwon Do to the heavyweight boxer Muhammad Ali and other famous people, and was the only Korean to be named one of the National Immigration Forum's most recognized immigrants.

North America is the home of many Koreans with diverse talents and skills: journalist K. W. Lee has made outstanding contributions to the mainstream and Korean American media; labor specialist Shinae Chun, director of the U.S. Department of Labor's Women's Bureau, became the highest-ranking Korean American in the administration of President George W. Bush; and concert pianist Lucille Chung, a second-generation Korean Canadian, performs with orchestras worldwide. Koreans are well represented in American hospitals and universities, and are increasingly becoming more visible in political circles.

Jhoon Rhee, called "the Father of American Tae Kwon Do," is one of the Korean American community's most distinguished members.

Korean Arts, Festivals, and Holidays

The arts provide an avenue through which Korean immigrants can preserve their culture and share it with their adopted countrymen and women. Miyoung Kim,

Traditional Korean dances, which continue to be performed in North America, include the Buddhist nun's dance.

founder of the Korean Dance Studies Society of Canada, takes her troupe not only to Korean establishments, but also to such events as the National Soccer Gala, the Toronto International Folk Festival, and the Celebrate Toronto Street Festival. Through these performances, people from many cultures are exposed to some of Korea's beautiful ancestral dances: the fan dance, the Buddhist nun's dance, the farmer's dance, the sword dance, and other, original works.

Poongmul, a form of traditional Korean drumming that was associated with planting and harvest ceremonies, originated on the Korean Peninsula about 2,000 years ago. Today, it is a popular connection to the homeland for Korean Americans and Korean Canadians and can be heard during various holidays and festivals.

The extent to which individual Korean Americans and Canadians celebrate traditional holidays and customs varies. Of the many Korean celebrations, however, three are most widely observed among the immigrants to North America.

The Lunar New Year is celebrated by Koreans as well as many other Asian communities. This holiday, which Koreans call Solnal, begins with solemn ceremony and ends with games and dances. As with many Korean observances, honoring ancestors and respecting elders play central roles in Solnal, which features a memorial service, traditional dress, and a presentation of younger family members to older ones. Members of the young generation bow to their elders, who respond with gifts of cakes, money, or fruit. Then it's time for games: traditionally, kite flying for boys and seesawing for girls. Everyone enjoys the farmer's dance, stepped to the sound of Korean drums and gongs.

For Korean Americans, Thanksgiving Day comes twice: on the fourth Thursday of November (the traditional American holiday) and on August 15, the Korean Thanksgiving, or Chusok. Chusok festivities actually begin on the night before and extend into the day after. As with the American holiday, Chusok is a time to express appreciation for all blessings and to

During celebrations of Chusok, the Korean Thanksgiving, gifts are commonly left at the graves of deceased family members.

Asian Produce Cropping Up on American Farms

New Jersey farmers take pride in their award-winning corn and tomatoes. Now they hope to harvest a bumper crop of accolades for Asian staples such as bok choy, mustard greens, and bitter melon.

As America's beleaguered farmers battle for survival, many are following immigration trends and growing products that will appeal to the relatively untapped ethnic market—and perhaps lead to financial success. "We can no longer grow products that can be produced elsewhere, so increasingly, our agriculture producers are turning to specialty crops and new emerging markets," said Tom Orton, a specialist at the Rutgers Cooperative Extension.

Rutgers' specialty crop initiative aims to introduce farmers to new produce and research marketability. So far, fruits and vegetables from eastern and central Asia have proven popular in New Jersey, an ethnically diverse state where 6 percent of the 8.4 million residents are Asian.

Farmers are selling most of their Asian products to small street markets and specialty stores, but Orton said these products should make their way to mainstream supermarket shelves soon. "We're going to see more of these landing in standard supermarkets in the near future," he said. "We know, based on marketing studies we've done, that people want options, more diversity. This is a great opportunity and we want to take advantage of it."

Adapted with permission from *Asian Diversity Magazine*.

get together with family. Traditional foods include rice cakes made with rice, beans, sesame seeds, and chestnuts.

The third holiday, Children's Day, is less widely observed, but it is fun for the young people nonetheless. On May 5, children honor their elders and ancestors and then enjoy traditional foods, games, and presents.

Koreans have a variety of cultural and social practices that differ from Western custom. Bowing to an older person is a sign of respect, and it is considered poor manners for a younger person to have direct eye contact with an elder. When Koreans enter a room, they remove their shoes. And just as 13 is considered to be an unlucky number in America, the number 4 represents death to Koreans.

A Blended Culture

There has been considerable dialogue among Korean Americans about which culture to embrace, Korean or American, with a middle ground emerging. Yet many practical problems exist for the offspring of Korean immigrants who wish to remain attuned to their family's heritage.

How can second-generation Korean Americans learn the language and culture of a country they have never visited? Their relatives are one source, but because many parents invest long hours in their businesses, Korean schools are a popular choice. These schools, which typically are held on weekends, offer instruction in Korean history and teach the Korean language. Many Korean schools also teach traditional music, art, and dance. One woman interviewed by the Voice of America sends her children to Korean school because, she says, "I want them to have a strong identity as a Korean American, not just another person born in the United States that has a different color skin."

Perpetual Guests?

Try as they might to adapt to life in the United States, some Korean Americans believe race is an issue that will prevent them from ever being fully accepted by mainstream society. The prejudice experienced by Korean Americans can be subtle or obvious. One disturbing attitude is that Koreans are merely temporary guests, foreigners eventually to return to the peninsula. Conversations that focus on a Korean American's race might be well intended, but they are also frequently condescending. Moon Jo, in *Korean Immigrants and the Challenge of Adjustment*, relates the experience of a Korean American man who has lived in Philadelphia for 30 years and meets another Philadelphian while traveling. "I am always happy to see a fellow Philadelphian," the man says. "Much to my surprise, the American-born Philadelphian could care less that I am from Philadelphia and went to school and work there. He is more interested in my nationality. When I tell him I was born in Korea and came to America when I was 13, he perks up and starts to tell me about a few Koreans he knows and how hard working they are. In spite of everything I have told him, I am a 'foreigner,' not a Philadelphian."

Another area where some Korean Americans report experiencing discrimination is the workplace. Today's employment laws prohibit practices such as not hiring a person because of his or her race. Yet, as sometimes happens with other minorities, Korean American employees may be treated as outsiders, making it more difficult for them to develop work-based social networks or mentors.

Korean American Women: They've Come a Long Way, Maybe

Many Koreans and Korean Americans were raised under the influence of the teachings of the ancient Chinese philosopher Confucius. While some of these tenets stand the test of time (the emphasis on education, for example), Confucian ideas about the role of women are in direct opposition to contemporary Western feminist thought. Consider Confucianism's three

Two-thirds of Korean American women hold jobs outside the home. Many also continue to perform the lion's share of domestic duties, in keeping with traditional Korean custom.

"obediences" for women: "to obey father at home, husband after marriage, and sons when widowed."

The traditional Korean roles for men and women might have changed very slowly in the United States and Canada if not for one factor: the workplace. Historically, homemaking is the primary role for a Korean woman, but immigrants who run small businesses quickly learn that both husband and wife are needed to make a profit or break even. About two-thirds of Korean American women have jobs, but especially for their husbands, gender-based habits are hard to break.

Researchers wondered whether Korean American women, with their new role as breadwinners, had fewer traditional responsibilities at home. Unfortunately for these women, not only could they "have it all," they were still expected to do it all. As Pyong Gap Min notes in *Korean American Women: From Tradition to Modern Feminism*, "Korean working wives' share of responsibility in the four major traditional domestic tasks [cooking, dishwashing, laundry, and housecleaning] is substantially lower than that of Korean housewives. However, Korean working wives still shoulder most household work, except garbage disposal." When other family members pitched in, they were most likely to be female. Summarizes Min, "Most Korean immigrant wives do work both in and outside of their homes and expect to do so, contradicting the myth that women will be cared for by men and that homemade gourmet foods and 'womanly' characteristics and appearances are the routes to a happy life."

6 WAKING UP FROM THE AMERICAN DREAM

The American Dream—that any person with an idea and hard work can succeed in the United States—has attracted many immigrants, including Koreans. For many, the dream has come true. For others, however, the "land of opportunity" has not lived up to its name. Some of the problems confronting Korean Americans are common to all immigrant groups, while others are unique to immigrants from the Korean Peninsula.

Generation Gaps

Since time immemorial, each succeeding generation has claimed to be different from the one that came before. For Koreans living in North America, there's much truth to that claim. Second-generation Korean Americans were born in a land where English is the predominant language; they don't necessarily speak Korean well, if they know the language at all. The first generation has a tendency to isolate itself from mainstream American society; many first-generation Korean Americans are uncomfortable with Western culture, and some are unable to converse well in English.

In *Contemporary Asian American Communities*, Mary Yu Danico writes about the feelings and experiences of 1.5-generation Hawaiian Korean Americans she interviewed for a study. Overall, they were embarrassed by stereotypes of first-generation Hawaiian Korean Americans (hot tempered, money

◀A Korean American shopkeeper surveys the damage to her business in the aftermath of the 1992 Los Angeles riots. Widely referred to in the Korean American community as *Sa-I-Gu*—literally, 4-2-9, or April 29, after the day they began—the riots put an end to the dreams of a number of Korean immigrants.

hungry, and pushy). They were also alienated from the second generation, who did not share the sometimes-difficult experience of being "fresh off the boat," or "Fobby." They gravitated instead to other 1.5-generation Asian Americans or non-Koreans. "To avoid the stigma of being immigrants, many 1.5ers avoided contact with other Koreans who were overtly Korean or 'Fobby' and presented themselves as Korean American or local," Danico observes. "Thus, by disassociating from those who reminded them and others of the existing stereotypes of Korean Americans, they could avoid being perceived by the larger society as 'typical' Koreans."

Immigration has profoundly affected the Korean family. In a traditional Korean family, the father is indisputably the head of the household; the mother rarely works outside the home, devoting herself to her children. "Koreans have deep attachment to their mothers and can be reduced to tears recalling their devotion," writes Michael Breen. "A father is often more fondly remembered for the guidance he gave and the sacrifice he showed towards a noble cause, like Korean independence or democracy, than to what he invested in the family."

Once in North America, the Korean family often is forced to forsake its traditional, gender-based roles because of financial necessity. The wife, for the first time, might be needed to work outside the home, often in a family-run small business. When the wife works alongside her spouse, it may be a "subtle reminder that the husband cannot operate the business alone and is, therefore, somehow less a breadwinner, perhaps even a failure. That, in turn, can . . . lead to friction, arguments, and even fights or abuse," according to Moon Jo.

Korean American parents typically are willing to make tremendous personal sacrifices for their children, but often with the expectation of high academic achievement by their sons and daughters. While the children might understand and appreciate the long hours their parents put into their work so that they can have a better life, the academic demands can take a toll on the parent-child relationship. In *Becoming Asian*

The "Tweens"

To most Americans, a "tween" is someone who is between the ages of 10 and 12—not a little kid, not a teenager. One research study describes a different type of tween: young Korean Americans caught between two cultures.

In "A Generation in Transition: A Study of Korean-American Youth," two Eastern College researchers, Charlie Swan and Jill Weissbrot, explore how some Korean American teens view their cultural identity. The researchers spent two months observing and interacting with about 25 members of a Korean American church youth group, 7 of whom were part of a smaller focus group.

While these children of Korean-born parents embraced the value Koreans place on family and appreciated the sacrifices their parents made for them, "they were beginning to judge Korean customs [such as bowing to an elder] by the standards of American culture." One youth said, "You have both cultures kind of mixing in, and they don't really mix that well."

Rather than choosing one culture over the other, the researchers note, the subjects of their study "found self-definition and support through their relationships with other Korean American youth, who were experiencing these same vital conflicts and changes." In other words, the Korean American tweens relied on one another to develop a blended world of their own.

American, a Korean American named Cori talks about her parents. "I was a B student in an A+ household. I had fights all the time with my parents about grades and other things," Cori said. "They took it almost like a sign of disrespect to them, if you didn't get straight A's. . . . I'm really glad they taught me the importance of education and doing the very best at whatever you do. That's a valuable part of Korean culture and I want to hold on to it. But there are other things that are as important as schoolwork, like knowing how to socialize with people, how to get a point across well in a conversation."

Some Korean American parents worry that their sons and daughters are becoming too independent, too "Americanized." But these concerns eventually might go beyond whether children seek their parents' advice or try to please them by getting good grades. The traditional Korean custom of children taking care of their aging parents appears to be on the decline in America. In one study of adult Korean Americans, most of the respondents said their marital relationship was more important than their relationship with their elderly parents. For Korean American seniors, that could mean more years in the workforce. A 63-year-old restaurant owner told author Moon Jo, "By this time I was going to retire, but I can't do that now. I don't have much savings, and I don't think I can ask for any kind of financial help from my children, even though they are fairly well off."

The Shadows of Stereotypes

The 1.5-generation Hawaiian Korean Americans in Danico's study felt they were stereotyped unfairly. They aren't alone. Korean Americans are lumped together with other Asian Americans as being the "model minority"—smart, silent, submissive, and prosperous.

"Many people think that all Koreans go to Harvard and get A-pluses, that all Koreans are rich," said Paul Kim, a Los

Comedian and *Tonight Show* host Jay Leno ignited a firestorm of indignation within the Korean American community by alluding to the increasingly uncommon practice of eating dogs.

Angeles police officer, in *East to America*. "This [the Los Angeles Korean] community has a lot of tragedies, a lot of stereotyping in reverse. We have a lot of poor and uneducated people."

In 2002 talk show host and comedian Jay Leno found himself embroiled in controversy after joking that a disqualified Korean Olympic speed skater "kicked his dog and ate it." Not only were Koreans upset by Leno's humor, but Korean Americans were worried that others would think they participated in what one Korean American described as "the declining cultural practice of eating dogs." During a nearly 30-minute phone call with Charles Kim, the executive director of the Korean American Coalition, Leno said he had only meant to make people laugh and that he had "checked out whether or not Koreans actually ate dogs." The response of NBC, which airs Leno's program, was, "By its nature, comedy can be impolite, and the humor on 'The Tonight Show' is no exception. People can have different opinions about where the lines should be drawn."

Human Trafficking

The smuggling of human beings across national boundaries for the purpose of forced labor or prostitution is a global problem. Of the approximately 700,000 people worldwide who were sold for labor or prostitution in 2002, about 50,000 were taken to the United States.

The U.S. Department of State considers the Republic of Korea to be a "Tier 1" nation, meaning that South Korea complies fully with the standards established in the Victims of Trafficking and Violence Protection Act of 2000. To that end, South Korea established an Interagency Committee for Countermeasures to Prevent Trafficking in Persons in 2001 and has developed a public education campaign.

However, Koreans still are being taken to the United States and Japan for forced labor or prostitution. In March 2001, for example, Canadian police broke up a human trafficking ring.

The traffickers were accused of charging North Korean, South Korean, and Chinese people thousands of dollars each for passage to North America, then trafficking them to others who would make them work without pay or sell them for sexual activities. The victims entered Canada as tourists and then were smuggled into the United States. According to police, the ring smuggled nearly 1,200 people in the course of one year.

Immigrants can fall victim to fraud. In 2003 the *Los Angeles Times* reported the story of a U.S. immigration official who took bribes in exchange for issuing authorized permanent resident cards. In this scam, the green cards, which enable non-citizens to live and work legally in the United States, were issued to Koreans living without proper documents in California. Although the immigrants said they were unaware of the illegal activity—they thought they were paying to have their cases for permanent status moved along faster—as of January 2003, officials were seeking them for deportation. One Korean man said, "We had our dreams of being American citizens, just like everybody else. We're good people. But now the government treats us like criminals. . . . Our only mistake was that we trusted people."

Caught in the Middle: Grocery Boycotts and the L.A. Riots

The rioting that exploded on April 29, 1992, in South Central Los Angeles changed the lives of a number of Korean immigrants in the United States. But beginning in the early 1980s, tensions were rising between African Americans and Korean Americans in major U.S. cities, including New York and Chicago.

The seemingly innocuous setting for many of these conflicts was the mainstay of Korean small businesses, the grocery store. Many of the markets were located in poor, primarily African American neighborhoods. The details differ from city to city, but a common pattern emerged: a disagreement or incident occurred between an African American customer and a Korean

American merchant; the incident became known throughout the neighborhood; the neighbors spontaneously protested in front of the store; and African American activists encouraged local citizens not to buy anything from the market. Generally the action ended in a matter of weeks or months, as in the case of the 1990 Church Avenue boycott in Flatbush, Brooklyn.

On the surface, these boycotts seemed to be the result of racial conflict between African Americans and Korean Americans. It wasn't one incident that fueled calls for a boycott, but rather ongoing poor customer relations. "Ostensibly, the black boycotts of Korean stores were launched to protest the 'disrespectful' treatment of black customers by Korean merchants and to demand racial justice," wrote Heon Cheol Lee in *Koreans in the Hood: Conflict with African Americans.* "The chant 'no respect, no money' was a constant refrain at picket lines in front of stores or at black unity rallies."

For their part, some Korean Americans said the store owners' seeming lack of friendliness was in part culturally instilled, in part a manifestation of exhaustion from working 14-hour days. As one Korean explained, "Western culture is very open. It is kind, always smiling, that is the tradition. But we are very different. If a Korean woman smiles at an unknown man, we would think she is a prostitute. Even if they don't smile, it is not their intention to be rude or arrogant . . . they are trained not to smile."

Another theory offered to explain conflict between African Americans and Korean Americans is the notion of the "middleman minority." According to this theory, a wide gulf exists between poor minorities and large corporations, and it rankles many urban poor when companies make a profit off them but do not reinvest in the community. The merchants who buy goods from the large companies and then sell them to minorities are caught in the middle. They become the focus of their customers' discontent, even if they are minorities themselves. The theory "explains why Jews, Italians, and now Koreans are disliked, even hated, by minority residents . . . [who] transfer their dislike of the corporation to the middleman minority," notes Moon Jo.

In urban centers, African Americans are frequently not the predominant business owners. Sociologist Jennifer Lee, in *Civility in the City: Blacks, Jews, and Koreans in Urban America*, captures the frustrations of one West Harlem man: "Like I tell you, there's no black-owned businesses up here. Everybody that comes here, every nationality is always put before us. . . . Every newsstand you see is Indian owned and all the medallion cabs too. You got your Korean restaurants, your Indian newsstands, your Greek or whatever frank stands. What do you have here that's black, except for maybe something on 125th Street?"

Some African Americans also think that other minority business owners get preferential treatment. In Lee's field research, 60 percent of the African Americans believed Korean and Jewish businesspeople received special loans or tax breaks. In reality, none of the Korean businesspeople in Lee's sample financed their business through bank or government loans.

Often the African American boycotts of Korean grocery stores were organized by activists from outside the immediate neighborhood, bolstering the argument that the actions were about more than relations between African Americans and Korean Americans. During the Church Avenue boycott, African Americans shopped at other Korean-owned stores, and some even tried to enter the grocery store in question. After the boycotts ended, many of the African American customers returned.

In *Civility in the City*, author Jennifer Lee says, "The boycotts garnered both local and national media attention, giving black nationalist leaders a forum in which to propagate the broader issue of black control over black communities." That control is not only economic in nature, suggests Heon Cheol Lee, but political as well.

As African American–led protests and boycotts of Korean stores were occurring throughout the United States, the stage was being set for the riots in Los Angeles. On March 3, 1991,

A videotaped sequence, captured by a man on the balcony of a nearby apartment and repeatedly broadcast by television news programs, appeared to provide convincing evidence that four white Los Angeles police officers had used excessive force in arresting black suspect Rodney King after a high-speed car chase on March 3, 1991.

a black man named Rodney King was severely beaten and kicked by four Los Angeles police officers after a high-speed car chase. A person in a nearby building captured the beating on videotape. Although King sustained 11 fractures to the skull, the official police report did not reflect that he had been seriously injured. In large part because of the videotape—which was widely aired, both locally and nationally, by television news organizations—the officers were arrested on charges of using excessive force and assault with a deadly weapon.

In a separate incident, the Korean owner of an inner-city

grocery store in Los Angeles, Soon Ja Du, shot and killed 15-year-old Latasha Harlins over an allegedly stolen carton of orange juice. Du claimed she was acting in self-defense (though the girl was shot in the back of the head). Although convicted of manslaughter, Du received a sentence of five years' probation, community service, and a fine; she did not serve any jail time.

Following the Du trial, which greatly upset many African Americans in Los Angeles, the four officers arrested for the Rodney King beating had their day in court. On April 29, 1992, a white jury found the four officers not guilty. The response to the King verdict was swift and furious. African Americans and Latinos took to the streets of South Central Los Angeles that evening, looting stores and setting fire to buildings and automobiles. The rioting continued for three days, leaving 2,383 people injured and 54 dead. Of the 4,500 businesses destroyed or damaged, about 2,300 were owned by Korean Americans.

Violence and destruction engulfed South Central Los Angeles following the April 29, 1992, not guilty verdicts in the Rodney King police brutality trial. The riots exposed long-simmering resentments between blacks and Korean American business owners.

The family of Edward Song Lee at his funeral. Lee, attacked while trying to protect a Korean restaurant from a mob of looters, was among the 54 people killed during the L.A. riots—an event that some Korean Americans say continues to affect their view of the United States.

Why did black rioters target so many Korean businesses? Some in the media pointed to frayed relations between the Korean and African American communities. At best, however, this is a partial explanation. The very fact that Koreans owned a large proportion of the businesses in the South Central area made those businesses most vulnerable to destruction. And the consensus among experts is that the L.A. riots were fueled by a whole constellation of long-standing social and economic frustrations among African Americans.

But for a large number of Korean American business owners in Los Angeles, the riots spelled the end of their American Dream. A survey by the Korean American Inter-Agency Council found that fewer than 30 percent of Korean American businesses had reopened 10 months after the riots. Many of these Korean Americans moved out of the L.A. area, leaving their ruined stores—which represented years of hard work—behind.

After disaster comes rebuilding, and the Los Angeles community has been attempting to create not just new physical structures but new relationships. On the 10th anniversary of the riots, residents of L.A. held vigils and lit unity candles. African Americans and Korean Americans said that they were committed to learning the lessons of the past. But not everyone is convinced that enough has been done to effect lasting change. In a *Los Angeles Times* article, Edward T. Chang, a professor at the University of California-Riverside, said, "We've put race relations on the back burner and buried it. Underlying socioeconomic factors that ignited the riots haven't changed at all." A man living in the South Central neighborhood agreed. "Nothing," he said, "has changed. Why don't you come here at 6 o'clock, when the sun goes down, and see reality?"

If anything positive for the Korean American community emerged from the riots, it was a movement toward greater political and civic involvement. "There was a definable surge in Korean American political participation after the riots," claimed Nancy Abelmann and John Lie, the authors of *Blue Dreams: Korean Americans and the Los Angeles Riots*. "Several young Korean Americans we met were so deeply affected that they quit or abandoned plans for more lucrative jobs to enter community service—as representatives of Korean American organizations, volunteers in advocacy groups, or staff members of community organizations."

Welcome Back

Korea's strong economy and stable political status are two compelling reasons Korean Americans and Canadians have been drawn back to the peninsula. The attractiveness of living in the United States might also have faded for Koreans in light of difficult economic times, problems acclimating to a new culture, and fears of racial tension.

Fewer Koreans have been coming to the United States since the late 1980s, but interestingly, many have been returning to Korea. When Korea hosted the 1988 Summer Olympic Games, Koreans overseas saw a more attractive, progressive nation than the one they had left in the 1960s or 1970s. Among Koreans living in the United States, the Olympics jump-started an increase in reverse migration (returning to live in the country from which one previously emigrated). Only about 800 Koreans returned to Korea in 1980; by the mid-1990s, that number had reached about 5,000 each year.

7 THE FUTURE OF THE KOREANS IN NORTH AMERICA

Koreans have now lived in North America for more than 100 years. Although immigration laws and racially based quota systems limited their numbers in the first half of the 20th century, the immigration reforms of the 1960s—in both the United States and Canada—offered new opportunities for Koreans.

The U.S. census of 2000 counted more than 1 million people of Korean descent. The largest individual years for Korean immigration to the United States may be in the past, however. During the 1990s, a total of 164,166 Koreans arrived on U.S. shores. The figures for the 1970s and 1980s were 267,638 and 333,746, respectively.

Meanwhile, Korean immigration to Canada was on the rise. A total of 43,391 Koreans arrived in Canada during the 1990s—more than two and a half times as many as had made Canada their new home in either of the previous two decades. Nevertheless, in total numbers the United States remains a far more popular destination for Korean immigrants.

The Ramifications of Reunification

It is the fervent hope of Koreans everywhere that the peninsula, politically divided for more than half a century, will someday be reunified. Many Korean Americans have a very personal stake in reunification: according to one estimate, up to 500,000 of them have relatives living in North Korea whom

◀ Residents of Seoul demonstrate against North Korea's announced decision to restart its nuclear reactor and, possibly, create plutonium for atomic weapons, March 1, 2003. Despite recent tensions over this and other issues, some observers believe that, in the long run, the Korean Peninsula will be reunified politically. What effect that might have on Korean immigration to North America remains unclear.

Oh, Canada!

Between 1991 and 2001—a period during which Korean immigration to the United States declined—the number of Koreans moving to Canada surged. In 2001, Canada welcomed 9,604 Korean immigrants; 10 years earlier that figure had stood at just 2,486.

One reason might be Canada's approach. "In Canada, all cultures are accepted as they are," says Edward Kim, an accountant and secretary of the Canada Korea Society in Toronto. "The United States has its melting pot." Add to that a good health-care system, high-quality education, established Korean communities in Toronto and Vancouver, and often an easier time entering Canada than the United States, and the sum is a thriving group of Korean communities that others want to join.

Kim arrived in Canada as a teenager in 1978, joining his married sister. Now, he's the father of two children, ages 15 and 12. Teaching them Korean values and culture, he says, can be an uphill battle, but after the family visited Kim's homeland a few years ago, the children realized they could be proud of their Korean heritage and their Canadian nationality.

As for Kim, while he is impressed with the strides Korea has made toward modernization—although perhaps at the cost of some traditional values—he is happy to be a Canadian. "Canadian society is much more relaxed," says Kim. "You have the freedom to be who you are."

they are currently unable to see.

In the near term, however, reunification seems unlikely. Tensions on the peninsula remain high—indeed, 50 years after the fighting ceased, North Korea and South Korea are still technically at war. And the two countries could hardly have charted a more different course politically and economically. South Korea, which has embraced democracy and free-market economics, enjoys a vibrant culture and remarkable prosperity. North Korea, by contrast, has known only the autocratic rule of two Communists, Kim Il-sung and his son, Kim Jong-il. North Korea's economy is in ruins, and it is one of the world's most isolated nations.

Yet it is precisely North Korea's abject failure that, some analysts believe, makes an eventual reunification probable. The

South Koreans, writes Michael Breen, "are the miracle-makers. The story here is one of healing and the North Koreans, unfortunately, took bad medicine, and are . . . in many ways worse off. . . . But one way or another, they will be grafted on to the new Korea that the South has created, either by a collapse and absorption or by a more friendly process."

It's difficult to predict what effect reunification might have on Korean immigration to the United States and Canada, or on the Korean communities already in North America. On the one hand, a united Korea might foster a spirit of optimism and national pride, which might convince prospective emigrants to remain on the peninsula—and immigrants to return. On the other hand, the burden of rebuilding and integrating the backward North could cause a drag on the South's economy, which in turn might spur increased emigration.

Restless Energy

When Korean Americans and Canadians welcome their fifth, sixth, and seventh generations and beyond, how far will they have come from their insular beginnings? Ty Pak, a novelist, shared his vision of the future in the *Korean Quarterly* newspaper: "I have absolutely no doubt about our people reaching the top. We have this demon driving us, this restless energy, that won't leave us alone, until we get there. . . . We simply can't fail, even if we wanted to."

Famous Korean Americans/Canadians

The Ahn Trio, classical musicians. "Classical Music Lives Ahn," proclaims the website of Maria, Lucia, and Angella Ahn, who play cello, piano, and violin, respectively. They've been called "classical musicians for the MTV Generation." The three sisters, born in Seoul, moved to the United States with their parents in 1981.

Juju Chang, journalist. Chang has worked for ABC News since 1987, covering presidential elections, the White House, and breaking news, such as the bombing of the U.S. embassy in Kenya. She has reported for *20/20* and anchored *World News This Morning*.

Margaret Cho, comedian. A stand-up comedian since she was in her late teens, Cho starred in a television show, *All-American Girl*, and wrote and performed the plays *I'm the One That I Want* and *Notorious C.H.O.*

Yearn Hong Choi, poet and university professor. Choi came to the United States as a student in the late 1960s. He has a doctorate in political science and has been a university professor, but he also is an accomplished poet. Choi writes poems in English and Korean.

Sung Kwak, orchestra conductor. The maestro is music director of the Busan Philharmonic Orchestra and for several years held the same title with the Austin (Texas) Symphony. In the early 1970s, he was the conductor for the Joffrey Ballet in New York City. He has been a guest conductor with some of the world's best symphony orchestras.

Chang-Rae Lee, novelist. Lee's first book, *Native Speaker*, won the American Book Award and the PEN/Hemingway Award. He and his family immigrated to the United States in 1968.

Dr. Indong Oh, orthopedic surgeon. Oh, who came to America in 1970, has invented orthopedic devices that benefit people who need hip replacements. The recipient of 11 patents, he has developed three total hip replacement prosthesis systems.

FAMOUS KOREAN AMERICANS/CANADIANS

SuChin Pak, journalist. To many young people, Pak has one of the world's best jobs. As a news correspondent for MTV, she has interviewed such artists as Mary J. Blige and Billy Idol, and covered such serious news stories as the aftermath of 9/11.

Rick Yune, actor. He's qualified for the Olympics in the sport of Tae Kwon Do, modeled, and traded stocks, but Yune is best known for his movie roles. He portrayed Zao in the 2002 James Bond movie, *Die Another Day*. Yune was born in Washington, D.C., in 1971, the son of Korean immigrants.

GLOSSARY

amnesty: a pardon; the granting of legal status to an undocumented immigrant.

assimilation: the process by which a person from one culture takes on the mind-set, habits, and customs of another culture.

boycott: the refusal, usually by an organized group of people, to have commercial or other dealings with a person, store, or organization as a method of protest or persuasion.

emigrate: to leave one's country of origin to settle in another country.

entrepreneur: a person who starts a business.

first generation: with reference to Korean Americans, designates immigrants born in Korea who came to North America as adults. (Note: In general usage, the term *first generation* refers to the children of immigrants born in the new country.)

homogeneous: characterized by racial, ethnic, or cultural uniformity.

kye: a rotating credit club through which some Koreans accumulate the money to buy or start a business. *Kye* members contribute money to a "pool" on a regular basis, and participants take turns receiving the lump sum.

legal immigrants: people who become permanent residents of the United States and have the proper documentation.

melting pot: a place (as the United States) where different cultures blend together or immigrant groups assimilate into the broader society.

1.5 generation: Korean Americans who were born in Korea but immigrated to North America as children.

permanent resident card: a document issued to non-citizens that serves as proof that they are legally allowed to live and work in the United States; more commonly known as a "green card."

reverse migration: the return of immigrants to their country of origin.

GLOSSARY

second generation: with reference to Korean Americans, denotes the first generation of children born in the United States.

undocumented immigrant: a foreign-born person living in the United States illegally (without proper documents).

xenophobia: fear or hatred of foreigners.

FURTHER READING

Abelmann, Nancy, and John Lie. *Blue Dreams: Korean Americans and the Los Angeles Riots*. Cambridge, Mass.: Harvard University Press, 1995.

Breen, Michael. *The Koreans: Who They Are, What They Want, Where Their Future Lies.* New York: St. Martin's Press, 1998.

Jo, Moon H. *Korean Immigrants and the Challenge of Adjustment.* Westport, Conn.: Greenwood Press, 1999.

Kibria, Nazli. *Becoming Asian American: Second-Generation Chinese and Korean American Identities*. Baltimore and London: The Johns Hopkins University Press, 2002.

Kim, Elaine H., and Eui-Young Yu. *East to America: Korean American Life Stories.* New York: The New Press, 1996.

Kim, Kwang Chung, ed. *Koreans in the Hood: Conflict with African Americans*. Baltimore: The Johns Hopkins University Press, 1999.

Kwon, Ho-Youn; Kwang Chung Kim; and R. Stephen Warner, eds. *Korean Americans and Their Religions.* University Park: The Pennsylvania State University Press, 2001.

Lee, Jennifer. *Civility in the City*: *Blacks, Jews, and Koreans in Urban America.* Cambridge, Mass., and London: Harvard University Press, 2002.

Park, Kyeyoung. *The Korean American Dream: Immigrants and Small Business in New York City*. Ithaca, N.Y., and London: Cornell University Press, 1997.

Segal, Uma A. *A Framework for Immigration: Asians in the United States.* New York: Columbia University Press, 2002.

Võ, Linda Trinh, and Rick Bonus, eds. *Contemporary Asian American Communities: Intersections and Divergences.* Philadelphia: Temple University Press, 2002.

Zia, Helen. *Asian American Dreams—The Emergence of an American People*. New York: Farrar, Straus and Giroux, 2000.

INTERNET RESOURCES

http://www.bcis.gov

Website of the Bureau of Citizenship and Immigration Services.

http://www.asian-nation.org

C. N. Le, a Vietnamese-American sociologist, is the author of this site, which provides a comprehensive and informative analysis of trends and issues related to Asian immigrants.

http://www.koreancentennial.org

In 2003, Koreans and Americans celebrated a century of Korean immigration to the United States. This is the official website of the centennial celebration, with news stories, great links, and excerpts from letters written by the first Korean Americans, who arrived in Hawaii to work on the sugar plantations.

http://www.koreainfogate.com

This website provides information about Korean history and culture. A special tutor page uses Korean pop music to teach the language, and Cyber Tae Kwon Do makes learning about this traditional Korean martial art a virtual experience.

http://www.koreanquarterly.org

Written by Korean Americans, this award-winning online newspaper offers interesting insights into a very diverse community through features, personality profiles, book reviews, and more. Contains links to many sites pertaining to Korean adoptions.

http://icasinc.org

This is the website of the Institute for Corean-American Studies, a private research institution. Click on any of the symposium listings from the home page, and there's access to many thought-provoking presentations on Korean/Korean American issues made at the group's meetings.

INDEX

Numbers in ***bold italic*** refer to captions.

INDEX

INDEX

PICTURE CREDITS

CONTRIBUTORS

SENATOR EDWARD M. KENNEDY has represented Massachusetts in the United States Senate for more than 40 years. Kennedy serves on the Senate Judiciary Committee, where he is the senior Democrat on the Immigration Subcommittee. He currently is the ranking member on the Health, Education, Labor and Pensions Committee in the Senate, and also serves on the Armed Services Committee, where he is a member of the Senate Arms Control Observer Group. He is also a member of the Congressional Friends of Ireland and a trustee of the John F. Kennedy Center for the Performing Arts in Washington, D.C.

Throughout his career, Kennedy has fought for issues that benefit the citizens of Massachusetts and the nation, including the effort to bring quality health care to every American, education reform, raising the minimum wage, defending the rights of workers and their families, strengthening the civil rights laws, assisting individuals with disabilities, fighting for cleaner water and cleaner air, and protecting and strengthening Social Security and Medicare for senior citizens.

Kennedy is the youngest of nine children of Joseph P. and Rose Fitzgerald Kennedy, and is a graduate of Harvard University and the University of Virginia Law School. His home is in Hyannis Port, Massachusetts, where he lives with his wife, Victoria Reggie Kennedy, and children, Curran and Caroline. He also has three grown children, Kara, Edward Jr., and Patrick, and four grandchildren.

Senior consulting editor STUART ANDERSON served as Executive Associate Commissioner for Policy and Planning and Counselor to the Commissioner at the Immigration and Naturalization Service from August 2001 until January 2003. He spent four and a half years on Capitol Hill on the Senate Immigration Subcommittee, first for Senator Spencer Abraham and then as Staff Director of the subcommittee for Senator Sam Brownback. Prior to that, he was Director of Trade and Immigration Studies at the Cato Institute in Washington, D.C., where he produced reports on the history of immigrants in the military and the role of immigrants in high technology. He currently serves as Executive Director of the National Foundation for American Policy, a nonpartisan public policy research organization focused on trade, immigration, and international relations. He has an M.A. from Georgetown University and a B.A. in Political Science from Drew University. His articles have appeared in such publications as the *Wall Street Journal*, *New York Times*, and *Los Angeles Times*.

MARIAN L. SMITH served as the senior historian of the U.S. Immigration and Naturalization Service (INS) from 1988 to 2003, and is currently the immigration and naturalization historian within the Department of Homeland Security in Washington, D.C. She studies, publishes, and speaks on the history of the immigration agency and is active in the management of official 20th-century immigration records.

PETER HAMMERSCHMIDT is the First Secretary (Financial and Military Affairs) for the Permanent Mission of Canada to the United Nations. Before taking this position, he was a ministerial speechwriter and policy specialist for the Department of National

CONTRIBUTORS

Defence in Ottawa. Prior to joining the public service, he served as the Publications Director for the Canadian Institute of Strategic Studies in Toronto. He has a B.A. (Honours) in Political Studies from Queen's University, and an MScEcon in Strategic Studies from the University of Wales, Aberystwyth. He currently lives in New York, where in his spare time he operates a freelance editing and writing service, Wordschmidt Communications.

Manuscript reviewer ESTHER OLAVARRIA serves as General Counsel to Senator Edward M. Kennedy, ranking Democrat on the U.S. Senate Judiciary Committee, Subcommittee on Immigration. She is Senator Kennedy's primary advisor on immigration, nationality, and refugee legislation and policies. Prior to her current job, she practiced immigration law in Miami, Florida, working at several nonprofit organizations. She cofounded the Florida Immigrant Advocacy Center and served as managing attorney, supervising the direct service work of the organization and assisting in the advocacy work. She also worked at Legal Services of Greater Miami, as the directing attorney of the American Immigration Lawyers Association Pro Bono Project, and at the Haitian Refugee Center, as a staff attorney. She clerked for a Florida state appellate court after graduating from the University of Florida Law School. She was born in Havana, Cuba, and raised in Florida.

Reviewer JANICE V. KAGUYUTAN is Senator Edward M. Kennedy's advisor on immigration, nationality, and refugee legislation and policies. Prior to working on Capitol Hill, Ms. Kaguyutan was a staff attorney at the NOW Legal Defense and Education Fund's Immigrant Women Program. Ms. Kaguyutan has written and trained extensively on the rights of immigrant victims of domestic violence, sexual assault, and human trafficking. Her previous work includes representing battered immigrant women in civil protection order, child support, divorce, and custody hearings, as well as representing immigrants before the Immigration and Naturalization Service on a variety of immigration matters.

SHEILA SMITH NOONAN is a writer from New Jersey. She has a B.A. in political science and journalism and graduated with honors from Douglass College, Rutgers University.